Phenomenology and
Analytical Philosophy

DUQUESNE STUDIES
Philosophical Series

28

PHENOMENOLOGY AND ANALYTICAL PHILOSOPHY

by

Cornelis A. van Peursen

Duquesne University Press, Pittsburgh, Pa.
Editions E. Nauwelaerts, Louvain

B
829.5
.P393
1972

Preface

Originally translated by Mr. Rex Ambler, the text of this book has been checked and amended by the undersigned and approved by the author, who has also used the opportunity to make a few additions to the work.

Wherever possible, English editions of works have been mentioned in the bibliographies. Dutch titles as a rule, have been omitted. Indexes have been added for the convenience of the reader.

Henry J. Koren

Contents

Chapter One

Introduction: The Two Poles of Contemporary Philosophy

THERE are currents in contemporary philosophy that have long been firmly channeled, but there are also others that still wildly overflow their provisional embankments. Among these more turbulent trends must be reckoned the movements of phenomenology and analytical philosophy. These two are the more conspicuous because of the contrast they form in today's philosophy and scientific methodology.

There are schools of thought which more or less continue traditions of the past, such as neo-Kantianism, neo-Thomism and neo-idealism; besides these, there are also groups of philosophers who claim to have arrived at new ways of thinking, even though these ways are sometimes rooted in ideas that began to develop in an earlier period. The most important of these modern philosophies are dialectical materialism, developed in the previous century by Karl Marx and others and now elaborated in the wider field of science and praxis; the new philosophy of science, which is now being established under the influence of recent developments in physics and biology; the existential philosophies which found their starting point in the concrete conditions of human existence; and the movements of phenomenology and analytical philosophy.

Dialectical materialism is the most self-contained of these schools of thought; it flows in an almost impervious channel. The philosophies of science are being developed in various and isolated areas; sometimes they seek entirely new paths, sometimes they ally themselves with the methodology of one or the other of the above-mentioned trends—dialectical materialism, analytical (and positivistic) philosophy and phenomenology—or strive for the renewal of an older philosophical movement such as vitalism. The existential philosophies, closely allied with modern literature, displayed at the outset in a variety of ways a vehement protest against the closed systems of idealism. In their further development they have made good use of the methodology of phenomenology.

Phenomenology and analytical philosophies (including logical positivism) reveal the sharpest methodological traits. At first, thinkers of both persuasions announced their ideas not as a comprehensive philosophy but as a new method of philosophy and science. Methodological reflection has continued to figure largely in the whole development of these two schools: philosophical assertions must continually undergo the test of their method. Both of them resemble in this respect the program once set out by Descartes in his DISCOURSE ON METHOD; they too wish to make a new beginning in philosophy. Unlike Descartes, however, both initiate the new beginning by renouncing the traditional questions of metaphysics. In this they resemble Kant; like him, both phenomenology and analytical philosophy choose to limit themselves to the phenomena of immediate experience. They too hope to discover in these phenomena certain structures which, on the one hand, restrict the scope of philosophical statements and, on the other, make it clear that the meaning of these phenomena doesn't lie in their factual "givenness" but in certain logical rules. Their mutual resemblance —and resemblance with Kant—goes further, as appears from their later development: they place philosophical analysis in the dimension of practical activity and so integrate theoretical investigation in praxis.

These structural resemblances of the two trends make it easier for us to see also their differences. The latter are indeed far-reaching; they go beyond the field of philosophy itself and constitute at present the most important controversy in contemporary philosophy and, as we hope will appear, also the most fruitful. By thus being able to grasp both schools of thought in terms of method, one can compare the contrasting standpoints of these schools more readily than those, for example, of analytical philosophy and existentialism. The comparison of these schools is also, in view of their wishing to begin anew and yet be in open development, more useful than that between systems that are ideologically closed and mutually antagonistic, such as dialectical materialism and idealism. In view of their influence on recent developments in scientific methodology, this comparison is also of importance in areas outside philosophy. Analytical and positivistic ideas have been evidently at work in the methodology of the natural sciences, biology, psychology and the social sciences, while phenomenological ideas have been at work in psychology and psychiatry, in studies in history and religion, and to some extent also in the social sciences and biology.

The contrast between phenomenology and analytical philosophy appears on the face of it to assume large proportions, partly of an irrational nature. These deserve to be mentioned if only to reduce the controversy to more structural proportions. There is, in the first instance, a difference in mentality. However convinced either side may be of the certainty and objectivity of its own method, the phenomenological method appears to analytic philosophers as too fantastic and intuitive, irrational and incapable of proof, while the positive method of analytical philosophers strikes phenomenologists as a euphemism for the poverty of a philosophy which eliminates itself by its exclusive preoccupation with measuring, weighing and testing, supplemented by a series of tautological rules. From a psychological standpoint, this contrast may be described, as occasionally it is, in terms of emotional and intellectual types, or of the artistically gifted and the soberly flegmatic. Geographically, the contrast may be described as that between continental European and Anglo-Saxon philosophy.

Descriptions of this kind have the advantage of showing how it is that one tends, on account of one's mentality or on account of the country one happens to belong to and of the philosophy there prevalent, to ally oneself with one of these schools. Thus even a false description can be of some use; for it would be wrong to take this characterization of the two trends as definitive. Husserl's phenomenology displays rationalistic features—he has even been rejected by some left-wing existentialists as a dangerously rationalistic thinker. On the other hand, there are also analytical philosophers who recognize emotion as fundamental to philosophical reflection.

Geographical considerations are more to the point, but they conceal a deeper contrast, namely, that between the older philosophical traditions. We may recall, further, that contemporary analytical philosophy has been strongly influenced by the positivism of the Vienna Circle, at the heart of the European continent, while at the present time it is prevalent not only in Great Britain but also in Scandinavia. In the United States representatives of both schools are to be found, even among scientists, and the same can be said of some countries like Italy and the Netherlands.

Yet the geographical contrast still appears on the face of it to be the most striking of all. The number of phenomenologically-minded thinkers in Great Britain, for example, is extremely small, while analytical thinkers are almost as rare in France and Germany and have but little influence. It is only a few years ago that the German-speaking Ludwig Wittgenstein was brought again to the notice of the German public by a German edition of his work; the edition contained explanatory notes and, moreover, was preceded by an introduction which had to present him as an extreme existentialist. The French don't like to call a philosopher a "positivist" because they associate this term with superficiality and view it as even more opprobrious than "idealist" is among Anglo-Saxons, who have used that word more than once against phenomenology.

Better progress is made if the contrast between these schools is traced back to philosophical traditions. It is after all a question of contrasts in method, and this is by no means a coincidence in philosophy, for all actual divergencies in the history of thought have been co-determined by such methodic contrasts. The only reservation one needs to make in this characterization is that the concern of both schools is precisely to effect a renewal of method and, therefore, cannot be fully defined in terms of the past. Besides, a large number of classical contrasts needs to be produced in order to disclose at each point the asserted resemblance to earlier controversies.

Such a comparative procedure is most useful if one goes on to observe—as we hope to do in our analyses—how nevertheless the structure of phenomenology and analytical philosophy deviates from those very traditional contrasts and sometimes even overcomes them. A first example is the contrast between realism and nominalism. Phenomenology shows traits of the old realistic conception that general meanings have to some extent an existence of their own, apart from the judgments in which they are expressed. But Husserl himself had already broken with this conception; he sought a logical function which is active behind the judgments and constitutes meanings. Analytical philosophy, on the other hand, has many features in common with the older nominalism: meanings do not exist in themselves but issue from certain logical operations. Again, however, this leads to consequences that depart from traditional nominalism.

In a similar way one can cite other classical contrasts having the *prima facie* appearance of being precisely the differences at issue between phenomenology and analytical philosophy. For example, the epistemological quarrel between rationalism and empiricism still plays a role. Rationalism, to be found mostly among continental European thinkers like Descartes, Spinoza and Leibniz, views the intellect as the most significant factor in the acquisition of knowledge. According to many rationalists, the senses merely provide the raw material which the intellect then transforms into rational knowledge. Often associated with this is the view that there are certain concepts or categories independent of, or prior to experience that are responsible for the formation of knowledge. The function of knowing is then that of bringing together material that of itself is wholly chaotic. On the other hand, empiricism, to be found for the most part among Anglo-Saxons like Locke, Berkeley, Hume and Stuart Mill, views sense experience as the most significant factor in the process of knowing. Knowledge doesn't precede experience, it is not *a priori* but *a posteriori*. The primary function of knowing is to analyze what is given in experience. Phenomenology displays features of the rationalist tradition, and analytical philosophy of the empiricist, even if there are considerable differences; for example, analytical philosophy recognizes the possibility of clarifying knowledge independently of experience, as in logical analysis.

The final contrast that may clarify the issue is that between idealism and pragmatism. Phenomenology concerns itself with the ideal factor in the process of knowledge, in particular the activity of the "I," while analytical philosophy rejects the ideal as a standard and puts the stress on usefulness as the criterion. But here again phenomenology is in no sense equivalent to idealism, and analytical philosophy is not at all equivalent to pragmatism.

The contrast may also be summed up in terms employed by the two schools themselves. Phenomenology can then be characterized as transcendental, and the analytical trend as linguistic philosophy. A transcendental analysis is not concerned with the transcendental as such, with that which lies beyond experience, but with that which lies before it, with those conditions which make statements about phenomena possible in science as well as in ordinary language. Linguistic analysis doesn't concern itself merely with the meanings of words and the uses of language, but with the rules that govern those meanings and become visible in those uses. Although phenomenology can hardly be equated with everything in history that goes by the name of transcendental philosophy, whether idealist or realist in tone, it has this at least in common with it: it analyzes the knowing subject's contribution to knowledge. With Husserl this becomes explicit only in the second phase of his phenomenology, although it was implied from the beginning. Analytical philosophy, on the other hand, is not as a whole equivalent to that trend in philosophy known more strictly as linguistic analysis, but all the various trends in the analytical tradition come together at this point: they analyze the object's contribution to knowledge, by investigating logical rules and linguistic structures, syntax and grammar.

The attention, then, devoted respectively to the subjective pole and the objective pole in the field of knowledge in no way eliminates components of the opposite pole. In an early stage of his development Husserl developed an objectivism of meanings, the doctrine that meanings exist in themselves; many analytical philosophers, on the other hand, have devoted much time to analyzing so-called private experiences, analyzing, that is, subjective language, such as "I feel pain," as well as words related to the subjective pole, such as "I," "here," "now." These movements closely resemble each other insofar as both map out structures of a logical nature, that is to say, structures that are not exhausted in what is factually given, whether physically, as in a material thing or verbal symbol, or psychologically, as in a process of thought or the experience of a meaning.

As this becomes clear in the chapters that follow, it will at the same time be seen that these structures have come to be viewed more and more in dynamic terms. The structures are not simply there; they are at work, they become visible. The center of gravity of this logical process can be situated variously: with the phenomenologists in the subjective pole, with the analytical philosophers in the objective pole. We find here again the distinction mentioned as characteristic of transcendental and linguistic philosophy, as well as the contrasts earlier spoken of. For the phenomenological method indicates an *a priori* and synthetizing procedure designed to draw attention to the subject's role, while the linguistic-analytic method points to an *a posteriori* and analytical activity. All this should be understood, of course, with the reserve of which we have already spoken.

One of the most important features the two trends have in common is that, as we said at the beginning of this chapter, they are still strongly fluid. Both contain "moments" that could easily have led to their ultimate fixation. Phenomenology at the outset could easily have become a realistic philosophy with a fixed scheme of "levels" (*Schichten*) and later have developed into a kind of idealism. Analytical philosophy, especially in the form of logical positivism, could have become a fairly dogmatic system in which meaningless metaphysical statements were sharply distinguished from logical and simply verifiable statements. There exist indeed offshoots of both systems that have come to such a fixation. Yet both movements contain deeper motives which press for unceasing renewal and transformation. These motives lie in the tension which arises when a philosopher endeavors to perform the purest possible analysis without losing sight of the particularity of concrete phenomena. For whenever the question of validity, the *questio iuris*, is put in a par with the question of the factual state of affairs, the *questio facti*, so that neither is sacrificed to the other, there must follow a continual confrontation in which the *questio iuris* and the *questio facti* interact incessantly. To bring this tension to light is one of the purposes of this book.

Despite all the divergences, then, between these two trends of thought, their convergence also will make itself felt. Both maintain that the sciences leave room for clarification by philosophy, because philosophy doesn't concern itself with the description of factual processes of, say, a physical or a psychical nature, but with the significance and meaning such processes may have. A chemical analysis of the spots made by printer's ink tells us nothing about the meaning of the printed words; a detailed historical description of the remains of cultural products is inadequate for the understanding of the symbolic function of human culture. In a similar way, a philosophical analysis must go beyond the search for facts to the discovery of logical structures, without which nothing like meaning or interconnection can come about. How important for the method of both philosophies is the distinction between a level of factual analysis (*questio facti*) and a level of logical analysis (*questio iuris*) will appear in the following chapters. It should also become clear how questions of fact nevertheless affect logical analysis, how they lead as it were to points of friction which compel further development, refinement of meaning and revision of logical boundaries. A logical analysis which has no contact with such a level of friction is like a machine turning idle, as thinkers of the later phase of analytical philosophy say. This implies that the question of validity is not to be isolated so as to degenerate into self-justification—which is the background of every form of petrified absolutism, whether it be idealist or positivist.

This converging tendency manifesting itself in both trends is not unrelated to the broader landscape of contemporary philosophy. We may briefly note here that an analogous tension reveals itself in philosophers of other persuasions. For example, the so-called dialectical school in the philosophy of science has as one of its themes the restless interplay and interlocking of the *a priori* and the *a posteriori* elements of knowledge: what is called "fact" and "experience" is from the outset determined by rules in terms of which these are grasped; conversely "knowledge" and "reason" are in confrontation with this experience. P. Barnays, F. Gonseth and G. Bachelard may be counted in this category. The work of Jean Piaget in psychology and logic also displays this tendency. All these thinkers have been very influential especially in France and Switzerland. In the Anglo-Saxon world Findlay occupies a position of his own: he is developing a philosophy in which elements of idealism and of analytical philosophy are evenly balanced. In another direction one finds in M. Polanyi and the thinkers influenced by him this element of confrontation and of dialectic whereby he discovers behind the descriptive language of science the personal language of commitment. The work of a thinker like Charles Perelman of Belgium points in the same direction: he lays the stress on rhetoric, the language of persuasion. In the later phase of linguistic analysis the same element comes to the fore, as we will see in Chapter Ten.

An introductory chapter must also pay attention to the rise of phenomenology and analytical philosophy, a subject which of itself would deserve a monograph. The term "phenomenology" was coined earlier in philosophy, appearing, for example, in Hegel, but owes its current usage to Husserl. For him phenomenology is the doctrine of phenomena; the term, however, is not used as in Plato and Kant in contradistinction from the real but hidden *noumena,* but as a designation of essences that actually reveal themselves as such. This attention to "what appears" terminologically implies a rejection of metaphysics. Later, the word "phenomenology" was used by thinkers influenced by Husserl, some of whom, such as Max Scheler and Nicolai Hartmann, tend to a metaphysical view. Nor is it always easy to differentiate between phenomenology and existentialism, which has made good use of the phenomenological method. This applies in particular to the works of Karl Jaspers and Martin Heidegger, but we don't reckon them here as phenomenology because the principal theme of their thought—"Being," the transcendent—is not defined by the phenomenological method. The case is different with Maurice Merleau-Ponty, who maintains the phenomenological approach in his ultimate themes, although in so doing he thoroughly revises the meaning of the word "phenomenology."

The name of the other movement—neo-positivism, analytical philosophy or linguistic analysis—is less definite. This movement actually comprehends several different schools and also various individual thinkers who do not wish to be classified at all. Even if one resorts to the distinction between trends of thought that subsequently arose, such as logical atomism, logical positivism and linguistic analysis, one has to take into account that some lines of development run parallel but have only occasional interconnections. For example, Moore's style of analyzing the meaning of ordinary language finds further application in Wittgenstein's work as well as, more or less independently, in the studies of Austin. For this reason it is more difficult to describe neo-positivism as one philosophical movement than is the case with phenomenology. Yet, the various trends retain an unmistakable "family resemblance."

In more recent writings the terms "linguistic philosophy" and "analytical philosophy" are often used for the whole movement, since the difference with the older positivism is considered to lie in the substitution of the analysis of the elementary structures of language for that of the elementary positive data of reality. That is to say, analytical philosophy is considered to have started with the transition from a "material" manner of speaking (about simple elements or immediate sense-impressions) to a "formal" manner of speaking (about the simple meanings of words or meaningful statements). In this sense, positivists such as Ernst Mach of Austria and Auguste Comte of France used a "material" manner of speaking, while neo-positivism as a whole is equivalent to what is indicated by a new term like "analytical philosophy."

A difficulty, however, lies in this that the term "linguistic analysis" also bears a narrower meaning and refers especially to those thinkers who limit their investigations to the analysis of the uses to which language is put. Even then the term is subject to dispute. G. Ryle refers to "linguistic analysis" as the term which writers on "the other side of the Atlantic"—at the moment of writing he happens himself to be on the right side, that is, in the British Isles —use to designate the more recent developments of British philosophical analysis. This indicates that there are different shades of opinion within analytical philosophy. It began originally with the necessity of reducing all statements to their verifiability in experience, together with the recognition of logical statements (i.e., tautologies, a term to be explained in Chapters Four and Five). It was spoken of by some as "logical empiricism"; by English authors mostly as "logical positivism," a term in which the bond with experience—the verification principle later to be discussed—received less emphasis. Two terms that commanded favor for a while were "physicalism"—an attempt of some logical positivists to translate all statements into the language of the physical sciences—and "logical atomism"—a doctrine that the structure of language portrayed that of reality, so that atomic constellations were reflected by atomic statements. But both terms refer only to phases in the development of logical positivism.

An important renewal took place when language was no longer considered to be bound to experience in such a simple way, but understood to function in a variety of ways, in other words, to be more than a merely empirical description or purely logical language. A phase began that is generally known as "linguistic analysis," a somewhat narrow term since this phase is certainly not concerned with the analysis of linguistic problems. There is, indeed, one group of thinkers, exemplified by Austin, who confine themselves to trying out the possibilities implied in the use of language, so that these may well be called linguistic in the narrow sense. Others, however, deal in their analyses with wider philosophical problems; that's why one may also speak of this later phase as that of "analytical philosophy." In the chapters that follow the significance of all this will become clear; here we only mention the terminological distinctions.

Let us add a few remarks to place these two philosophies in historical perspective. Both phenomenology and analytical philosophy arose from a certain discontent with the existing philosophical systems precisely because they lagged behind the progress made in science. Husserl was a mathematician and at first had little interest in philosophy. Philosophy appeared to have played itself out; the discussions on realism and idealism had reached no solution; neo-Kantianism was dominant in many universities on the European continent and, beside it, one found at best a sceptically-minded positivism. The period was one of great spiritual fatigue. When Husserl had discovered philosophy for himself and developed an entirely new method in his phenomenological reduction, which he himself experienced as a great renewal, he wrote in 1935, in the midst of the threats of National Socialism: "Europe's greatest danger is fatigue." He also spoke of a new approach to introspection, and that is connection with a difficult argument on the phenomenological method.

His interest in philosophy was aroused by the lectures of Franz Brentano. Here was a kind of introspection in method: over against the genetic psychology that tried to elucidate psychological causality, Brentano presented a more fundamental descriptive psychology that tried first of all to define the psychological phenomena of internal experience, phenomena such as feeling, memory and will. One of the most important concepts that he thereby traced was that of intentionality. This term had already been used in scholastic philosophy, but Brentano used it to mark the distinction between physical, non-psychological phenomena and psychological phenomena. The latter, he held, were characterized by being directed toward something outside themselves. Intentionality is directedness (*Richtung*) toward an object; every psychical phenomenon is characterized by its object; for example, representation is characterized by the object which it represents. Such an object is not necessarily something real, but it intrinsically qualifies (*immanente Gegenständlichkeit*) the specific psychic act; for example, the act of imagining is qualified by its imaginary object. In this way describing the act is at the same time describing its object. Brentano also spoke of his method as descriptive phenomenology.

Husserl was influenced by him in many respects. However, it was precisely in his early development that he began to abandon Brentano's philosophy, which was mainly concerned with experience, internal experience, and which to that extent was empirical,

Over against this, Husserl became increasingly convinced that a logical, rather than empirical, description alone could furnish an explanation of phenomena. This led ultimately to his phenomenological reduction that was to compel him in due course to investigate introspection from an entirely new, that is, transcendental perspective. This too is one of the lines to be pursued in the following chapters.

Husserl's new approach, however, is already evident to some degree in his earliest, so-called pre-phenomenological period. At Halle, Husserl defended his thesis on the concept of number (1887), which was again taken up in his PHILOSOPHY OF ARITHMETIC, vol. 1 (1891). At the University of Halle Husserl worked under the supervision of Carl Stumpf. A disciple of Brentano, Stumpf recognized the physical and psychological or intentional phenomena of his master, but distinguished beside them a third realm, namely, that which forms the content of logical propositions. Such contents he called "states of affairs" (*Sachverhalte*), a term which was not only accepted among phenomenologists but also given a significant role in the work of Wittgenstein. Stumpf had also an intensive contact with the American philosopher William James; and, as Spiegelberg, the historian of phenomenology frequently points out, James' ideas were of importance to Husserl.

In his PHILOSOPHY OF ARITHMETIC Husserl attempted, by means of descriptive psychology, to reduce the concept of number to the act of counting. This implied, on the one hand, what Husserl was later to reject as "psychologism," that is, a reduction to psychological processes. On the other hand, it was an attempt to get behind something that appeared at first to be simply given, to look at it, as it were, from the viewpoint of an activity behind it. In a later period Husserl conceived this activity as logical (transcendental) rather than as psychological. The development from a description of empirical data to an analysis of logical structures forms the transition to Husserl's phenomenological period.

Among the people who influenced this transition we must name first of all Gottlob Frege, who sharply distinguished between logical and psychological explanations. This he did very cogently in his extremely critical judgment on Husserl's PHILOSOPHY OF ARITHMETIC.

It was erroneous, wrote Frege, to reduce the logical status of a statement to the sense of the representation, to reduce it to the psychological (in Frege's word, *Sinn*, empirical meaning). An assertion about the moon signified more than a psychological idea. "For would not the moon lie rather heavily on the stomach for our condition of consciousness?" he asked. One must therefore look for the logical sense, that is to say, the meaning (*Bedeutung*) to which a statement refers, for that is the matter in question, the "thing itself" (an expression later used frequently by Husserl).

In Husserl's LOGICAL INVESTIGATIONS traces of Frege's critique are clearly to be seen, as the following chapter will show. There, in the Prolegomena of the work, Husserl gave an ample critique of psychologism, the doctrine which derives logical validity from factual data, i.e., from psychological processes. By the second edition of this work there was a further adjustment: he had moved the center of gravity from a psychological analysis which was still too descriptive to one that attempted to indicate the "pure" essence of psychic phenomena. (By "pure" Husserl meant "logical.") The distinction that Frege had made between the sense of the empirically available expression (called by Frege *Sinn*, by Husserl *Bedeutung*) and the logical status of such an empirical sense (called by Frege *Bedeutung*, by Husserl *Gegenstand*) now appeared in Husserl too. This terminology is used also by Alexius Meinong and Ludwig Wittgenstein. An example of two different empirical senses with the same logical status would be: "the victor of Jena" and "the loser of Waterloo," both of which refer to Napoleon.

Another influence is that of Rudolf Lotze, the philosopher who had interpreted the Platonic ideas not as metaphysical realities but as that which was logically valid. Husserl combined this with ideas from a philosopher and logician who had long remained unknown, but who in recent times has attracted more attention: Bernhard Bolzano. Writing in the first half of the nineteenth century, Bolzano had even then drawn a line between logical and psychological investigations by speaking of independent truths and propositions (*Wahrheiten* and *Sätze an sich*) as the logical content of spoken judgments. By this and other logical distinctions Bolzano influenced thinkers like Brentano, Stumpf and Meinong. The philosophy that Meinong developed at Graz ran in many ways parallel to Husserl's early phenomenology. Meinong had contacts with foreign scholars also, as, for instance, with Bertrand Russell and G. E. Moore.

Some of these men set their eyes on the Leibnizian ideal of an all-embracing logic, in which logical truths (*vérités de raison*) were to be clearly distinguished from factual truths (*vérités de fait*). The conceptions and developments here simply mentioned can only be made clear in the chapters that follow. It will become evident also that phenomenology in particular has never given rise to a logic in the proper sense—such as we find in neo-positivist trends—though it is true that logical analysis has played a big part there and is continually being extended.

Another thinker of that time, whose work Husserl judged in some respects favorably, in others unfavorably, was Ernst Mach. His philosophy may be called positivist and is of great importance for the logical positivists. He stressed the pragmatic, "economic" character of thought and wished to reduce knowledge to the simplest elements of observation. As soon, however, as this "material" manner of speaking was transposed into a "formal" manner, the first step to logical positivism would have been taken. This happened in fact when a group of thinkers and scientists with an interest in logic endeavored to frame a philosophy which, by its logical structure and immediate verifiability in experience, did not have to yield to modern science. This group was the so-called Vienna Circle, which included M. Schlick, R. Carnap and O. Neurath. In Berlin there was a similar group, including H. Reichenbach and R. von Mises. Another influential thinker was Karl Popper, who worked in Austria and later in England. The Vienna Circle broke up in 1938 under the pressure of the Nazis, but many of its members continued their work in the United States and elsewhere.

A number of other thinkers has influenced this movement. In particular, the logical work of Bertrand Russell, undertaken in collaboration with Alfred North Whitehead and as an elaboration of Frege's ideas, was of tremendous significance. Important too was Russell's empirical approach to old philosophical questions, an approach which continued the lines of the British empiricism of

Locke, Berkeley and Hume, with a scientific orientation. Wittgenstein, one of the most important thinkers within analytical philosophy, was a student of Russell and, without belonging himself to the Vienna Circle, was able to exercise a profound influence on its ideas through personal contacts, as will appear especially in Chapter Five.

Behind the interest in logic was a concern to clarify the language of philosophy. In this attempt at clarification one may detect the influence of thinkers who, without being positivists, were trying in a new way to combine philosophy with linguistic analysis. Thus Fritz Mauthner, at the beginning of the century, devised a critique of language which, despite a positive analysis of word-meanings, had a negative outcome; for language ultimately turned out to be inadequate and, like a ladder no longer needed, had to be discarded. Wittgenstein's work displays Mauthner's influence at both points. The recognition of the negative aspect, unusual for logical positivism, may perhaps be explained by the work of Schopenhauer, who stressed the limitations of the human conceptual world and whom Wittgenstein himself had studied. In his NOTEBOOKS, his TRACTATUS and his PHILOSOPHICAL REMARKS (1929) Wittgenstein took over Schopenhauer's terminological distinction between "will" and "idea": the conceptual and mental world can be logically analyzed, but the will cannot be put into words (cf. Chapter Nine). And in his later development Wittgenstein advanced certain basic conceptions which, implicit in Schopenhauer, are reminiscent of Immanuel Kant.

Another thinker who pondered the meaning of language was G. E. Moore who, when he relinquished his chair in 1939, was succeeded by Wittgenstein. By a careful analysis of words such as "spirit," "observe" and "sense-datum," Moore refuted idealism, adopting a neo-realist rather than neo-positivist standpoint. He had undergone the influence of Meinong among others. It is important too that he investigated the meaning of the predicate "good," thus developing an ethics which has been influential in the most recent developments of linguistic analysis whenever this has concerned itself with ethical problems.

These influences contrived to turn the current of thought in analytical philosophy in another direction than that in phenomenology. Nevertheless, they have come close to each other at many points, as has been shown already. Moreover, in the working out of their respective themes there are similar tensions, as those between language and reality, between ordinary language and logic, between the question of validity, of *vérités de raison* and that of *vérités de fait*. In an attempt to overcome a certain weariness in philosophy, in which metaphysical expedients were abandoned, two philosophical trends emerged which endeavored with an unwearying sense of urgency to combine clarity of thought with the recognition of sometimes startling facts.

Brief Bibliography

G. Frege, "E. G. Husserl: Philosophie der Arithmetik," *Zeitschrift f. Philosophie und philos. Kritik*, vol. 103(1894).

———, *Die Grundlagen der Arithmetik*, Breslau, 1884; reprinted, Darmstadt, 1961.

J. Héring, "Edmund Husserl, Souvenirs et Réflexions," *Edmund Husserl, 1859-1959*, The Hague, 1959.

E. Husserl, *Philosophie der Arithmetik*, vol. I, Halle-Saale, 1891.

———, "Bericht über deutsche Schriften zur Logik (1895-1899)," *Archiv f. systematische Philosophie*, vol. 9(1903) and 10(1904).

———, "Erinnerungen an Franz Brentano," *Franz Brentano* ed. by O. Kraus, Munich, 1919.

———, "Personliche Aufzeichnungen," ausgegeben von W. Biemel, *Philosophy and Phenomenological Research*, vol. 16(1956).

W. Illeman, *Husserls vorphänomenologische Philosophie*, Leipzig, 1932.

C. I. Lewis, *Mind and the World Order*, New York, 1929.

A. Meinong, *Philosophenbriefe aus der wissenschaftlichen Korrespondenz von Alexius Meinong mit Fachgenossen seiner Zeit (1876-1920)*, ed. by R. Kindinger, Graz, 1965.

G. E. Moore, "The Refutation of Idealism," *Mind*, vol. 12(1903).

C. K. Ogden and I. A. Richards, *The Meaning of Meaning*, London, 1923.

B. Russell, "Critique of Meinongs 'Untersuchungen zur Gegenstandstheorie und Psychologie,'" (Leipzig 1904), *Mind,* vol. 14(1905).

————, *Mysticism and Logic and Other Essays,* London, 1918.

A. R. White, *G. E. Moore, A Critical Exposition,* Oxford, 1958.

Chapter Two

Phenomenology and the Problem of Meaning

Psychologism was a trend of thought that believed it possible to formulate the actual laws of thinking in such a way that the logical validity of judgments could be derived from them. The trend had a large following in the nineteenth and early in the twentieth centuries; Husserl, we saw, was originally influenced by it. But, just as Hume, who sought to reduce the laws of thought to the mechanism of psychologically describable associations, proved to be the stimulus for Kant's logical analysis of propositions implying universal validity, so the ideas of psychologism induced Husserl to embark on his logical investigations.

Psychologism saw the new science of psychology as a kind of physics of thought: even as physics had discovered in matter a certain conformity to law, for instance, the law of gravitation, so psychology could do the same for the mind. This would amount in fact to explaining the laws of logic, for the rules of logic were there to be seen in human thought, in what psychology considered to be its object of study. It is this that Husserl objected to and that he refuted in his comprehensive LOGICAL INVESTIGATIONS. He there maintains that two very distinct aspects of the process of thought are confused by psychologism. Besides the psychological, empirical aspect of the thought process there is the content, in the sense of meaning, of the process. If in mathematics, for instance, one wrote the equation $(a + b)(a - b) = a^2 - b^2$, one would not then be describing a factual process, but stating what was logically valid. If one said, however, that in order to arrive at the product of the sum of, and the difference between, two numbers, one had only to work out the difference between the squares, then that would be a factual and practical stipulation. These factual stipulations, practical instructions, subsidiary norms and the like can play a big role in the pursuit of science, but they are to be clearly distinguished from the validity of scientific statements. For such stipulations and instructions do not yet have a logical foundation but merely have a factual basis, that is to say, they are based on human nature; that's why Husserl calls them "anthropological." They may even have a physical basis as, for example, in the three-dimensional relations of factually given, physical space; conversely, the grouping of numbers in two dimensions, as in the teaching of arithmetic, on the blackboard or paper, calls for an arithmetical method quite different to that employed in the grouping of numbers directly in three dimensions. All this, however, should make no difference to arithmetical laws as such.

The distinction between the logical quality and the factual components of the process of thought Husserl tries to clarify in the example of a calculating machine. One may compare this with human thought provided that one is also aware of the two distinct aspects: the machine works entirely according to mechanical laws which enable the numerals to spring into place. The order and mutual relations of these numerals are not determined, however, by the laws of mechanics, but by those of arithmetic. One cannot explain the mechanical operation in terms of arithmetic any more than one can explain the relations displayed in arithmetical rules in terms of physics. So too in the process of human thought there is a sharp distinction between psychological rules referring to the factual process of thought, on the one hand (*Realgesetz*, real law), and logical rules concerning non-factual validity, on the other hand (*Idealgesetz*, ideal law).

In the first volume of his LOGICAL INVESTIGATIONS Husserl is chiefly concerned to contest psychologism; in the other volumes he offers his draft for a doctrine of logical meaning, disentangled from rules of fact. The fundamental error by psychologism is that it bases truth on the human constitution. This can lead to more than one untenable paradox. Take for example the statement, "If everyone perished, then no one would exist." The psychologist would wish to found such a logical proposition on the manner in which men happen to think. The logical necessity of such a proposition would then rest on the fact that men, in view of their psychological constitution, must at one time have considered such a proposition to be true, but that this could have also been otherwise if men had been constituted differently. That is to say that such a judgment would be founded on the fact of men's existence. Then the truth of the non-existence of men, as the proposition in question lays down, would rest on the existence of men who don't exist! It becomes quite clear that logical truth cannot be founded on facts.

Similar considerations apply to the attempt of psychologically-minded thinkers to reduce the basic laws of logic—for example, $A = A$ and $A \neq A$—to factual psychological laws. They quote with approval Stuart Mill's description of the principle of contradiction: "The original foundation of it I take to be, that Belief and Disbelief are two different mental states, excluding one another," and "Two assertions one of which denies what the other affirms cannot be thought together." Husserl is fundamentally opposed to this reduction of laws of thought to factual and psychological conditions. It is not a question of whether or not two propositions can be thought together in empirical consciousness. A correct formulation would be: A and non-A cannot be thought together in consciousness-as-such (*Bewustsein überhaupt*), so long as one doesn't mean by this term empirical consciousness, not even a metaphysical consciousness, but the rules determining consciousness in a logical sense. Then, however, a logical law is no longer to be defined in terms of consciousness; rather, "consciousness" is to be defined in terms of conformity to logical rules.

It is understandable that Husserl now has nothing but praise for the anti-psychologism of Frege, thus going back on the criticism he had brought against Frege's standpoint and adverting with emphasis to Frege's THE FOUNDATIONS OF ARITHMETIC (1884). Following Frege, Husserl speaks of a being directed to ideal essential laws, of an endowment proper to logic, which he calls "logical evidence." This concept of "evidence" has been fiercely attacked, especially from the side of logical positivism. As we shall see, this attack has not been wholly without grounds, though Husserl in his refutation of psychologism defined the term "evidence" with great caution and wished to remove it from the psychical to the logical sphere.

From Husserl's exposition of logical evidence in his later writings, such as CARTESIAN MEDITATIONS and more especially the last volume of his LOGICAL INVESTIGATIONS, it is clear that he takes a different line from Brentano's. Brentano distinguished between internal and external perception: with respect to the first there was evidence (the experience of one's own feelings, for example), but with respect to the second there was none (the observation of a chair, for example). Husserl, however, put internal and external perception on one level. In both cases one must distinguish between sense-data (*Sinneseinhalte*) and "apperception." Apperception is one of philosophy's classical notions and is often contrasted with perception. For Leibniz, for instance, apperception is a kind of concentration of the attention by which the perceptions acquire greater clarity and logical coherence. For Kant apperception is a preliminary condition for the clarity and unity of perceptions, involving the act of reflection. Husserl himself stresses the transcendental, that is, the logically conditioning, character of apperception. He doesn't consider perception and apperception as two data on one and the same level. "Perception" is related to the content of experience, "apperception" to the way in which this content is assimilated.

What Husserl means with apperception can be explained in this way. Many philosophers view things as they appear to us as collections of sense-data, but they are wrong, for I must conceive a series of sense-data *as* that-house-there, and another series of sense-data, psychic sensations, for example, I must conceive *as* this-pain-of-mine. Internal sensation has no special privilege in this respect because in this case too an activity is required to distinguish sensations as this or that. It is this activity which he designates by the term "apperception." It is, then, in terms of apperception that the question of evidence must be posed with respect to both external and internal perception. Even this will leave more subtle differences undiscussed, for the very distinction between external and internal perception is really not so simple. Husserl refers in this connection to the physical components of supposedly purely psychic sensations.

It must be made clear, however, at the outset that for Husserl "evidence" does not denote a psychological evidence. Stuart Mill, like the psychologically-minded German thinker Christoph Sigwart, had defined logic in psychological terms as a "philosophy of evidence." Logic then describes the conditions on which the subjective feeling of necessity may arise. Over against this idea Husserl emphasized the objective character of logical evidence. In this case evidence points to the logical status of a proposition and may even be contrary to "evidence" in the subjective sense, as, for example, a feeling of certainty or a blind conviction. One can see the logical evidence of the proposition of Pythagoras even though one may at that moment have forgotten the proof and though one may have no attendant feeling of certainty. One *knows* that something is true.

For Brentano intentionality was the relation between consciousness and its object. For Husserl it is more; it is a directing of attention or focussing of the mind, which embraces objectivity as such. We may speak then of logical evidence only where objectivity (as in the case of a house observed, a pain felt, or a mathematical proposition) is distinguished from psychological acts, which are directed toward an object. Such an objectivity can remain essentially the same in a variety of acts, such as memory, perception and expectation. Reason is constantly at work in the perceiving and thinking subject—"reason in actuality," as Husserl later formulated it in his FORMAL AND TRANSCENDENTAL LOGIC—although the object of such a direction of the mind obviously lies beyond the activity of the moment. This process of identifying objects reveals a definite consistency (*Einstimmigkeit*) throughout the various forms of perception and experience. This means, first, that this objectivity is specifically logical in nature, to be clearly distinguished from the psychological processes that bring it, as it were, to light; and second, that in order to grasp this logical validity—a validity that is independent of facts as such—there must be a certain activity of the subject, namely, what has already been spoken of as apperception.

The notion of "evidence" plays a role in many philosophies; for instance, that of Descartes and even that of Locke. It has often been described as an inner feeling of certainty which accompanies elementary and logically founded assertions or statements. In his earliest work Husserl frequently uses the notion of "evidence" in the sense that it is impossible to think something that is contrary to evident states of affairs. Thus one can understand that his theory of evidence has been understood as a subjective and emotional certainty. But as early as his LOGICAL INVESTIGATIONS it is already clear that "evidence" is identical with an objective logical necessity. This idea is fully in line with Husserl's above-mentioned use of the term "intentionality" as a directedness toward an object which is qualified by such an objective state of affairs. The stress must not be laid on "consciousness" but on the logical necessity by which evidence is characterized.

For Husserl, then, logical evidence is not bound up with the psychological experiences of the subject, for it would then be a question of "evidence" as feeling; rather logical evidence is connected with that objectivity that shows itself consistent in a variety of acts, such as perception and memory. It is not a question of what is psychologically "real," but of what becomes logically, i.e., "ideally," apparent in the psychological process of knowledge. Here Husserl speaks of an "identifying overlapping," the norm of which is logical consistency, as over against its opposite, logical contradiction. It is precisely because he speaks in terms of logical identification that Husserl can lay so much emphasis on the activity of the subject and can speak of a specific act in which something is conceived by means of a logical objectification (as, for example, where recollected symbols that had been written with chalk on the blackboard are conceived, without being associated with that particular moment or material, as simply "the proposition of Pythagoras"). It is therefore understandable that in his later work Husserl should pursue this line of thought and come to speak of the activity and even the achievement (*Leistung*) of the subject; and that, further, Husserl should describe such an insight into that which has logical validity not only in terms of analysis or, technically speaking, of an analytical judgment, but in terms of an identification, that is to say, a synthesis.

It should be said in this connection that logical evidence in this sense may also embrace certain percepts—that-house-there, for example—which can be identified in a number of acts, such as observing or remembering. For logical status is not to be confined to such things as mathematical propositions. This, however, may give rise to an objection. How can one use the word "evidence" in the logical sense in which Husserl intends it, when it is clear that one can be mistaken as to the object of such an evidence? Is that which was previously evident now, after the discovery of the mistake, no longer evident? And is this not in conflict with a logical concept of evidence? Husserl's answer to this is that the object itself—whether a thing or a state of affairs—is grasped by and, indeed, present in the evidence. So that the possibility of being mistaken about the logical object is precluded. A mistake concerns facts, not the object as such. It means that something has been wrongly attributed to the object—a mathematical proposition, the perception of something actually present, etc. Authentic evidence has then been misapplied. In other words, a mistake is possible with respect to an actual object, but not with respect to the object of a logical act. This also holds true for (putative) perception; "those palm-trees there" retains its validity as logical evidence even where this statement is misapplied, in a situation, that is, in which it proved to concern a mirage.

Three things should now have become clear. First, even in his views on "evidence" and "being mistaken," Husserl rejects every kind of psychologism. A mistake may well affect evidence in the psychological sense, but not the logical status of a statement as such. Second, in his investigations Husserl is concerned with the logical data. Instead of metaphysically speculating whether or not houses, charts, values, etc. actually exist, he analyzes meanings. He hopes thereby to return to what is given in immediate experience so as to extract the validity from factual data by means of a kind of logical intuition (*Wesensschau*). This comes to expression in his motto, "Back to the things themselves," which has sometimes been construed too realistically by certain disciples as a return to the world of factual data. His exposition of "evidence" as invulnerable by mistakes shows clearly that he is talking about the "things themselves" in the sense of logical data. It appears, thirdly, that Husserl sees logical evidence as the validity of a given proposition or percept being immediately present to consciousness. The object, grasped as evident, is itself present.

The point is important because Husserl thereby distinguishes, as did others of that time (e.g., Frege and Meinong), between the actual content of a judgment and that which may or may not attend it. What is he referring to here? Among other things, to "evidence" in the subjective psychological sense. Whether or not feelings of evidence attend a certain proposition in fact makes no difference to its logical status. More important, however, as an attendant phenomenon is what in a logical sense is called "true" or "false." Even this fails to add to or subtract from the content of a judgment. Whether the proposition, "The house in N Street in red," is true or false has nothing to do with the logical content of the proposition; it only says something about the relationship of the content to factual reality. This could be formulated as follows: the expressions "is" and "is not" are equally concerned with the same matter, namely, that which is logically (as distinct from empirically) asserted in a particular proposition. With respect to this so-called "intentional matter" no mistake is possible on the basis of the evidence.

Take the following sentences:

There are intelligent beings on Mars.

Are there intelligent beings on Mars?

I hope there are intelligent beings on Mars.

These sentences clearly refer to one and the same "intentional matter," even though the acts directed to this matter are qualitatively different. By calling the acts also "intentional," Husserl means that they are directed toward the intentional matter, regardless of whether this matter be real or ideal, true or false, possible or impossible. Husserl does not choose the word "act" to designate a special activity. He is aware of the objection, raised by the neo-Kantian philosopher Paul Natorp, that consciousness is too often described in the language of "action," where action proceeds from a subject as "agent." He points out, however, that he does not in the least wish to propagate the "mythology of activities"; he wishes rather to revert attention from psychological activity to intentional experience, where the emphasis falls on the logical.

Husserl describes phenomenology as an analysis of the validity (*Geltung*) of statements, including those of the sciences. Ryle, in his study on phenomenology (1932), describes this aspect of Husserl's theory as follows: "All sciences and all sorts of search for knowledge or probable opinion aim at establishing particular or general propositions. But whether in any particular case such a proposition is true or false, the analysis of what it means, or what would be the case if it were true, is different from and in principle prior to the discovery of what proves it or makes it probable." Philosophy should not be compared with empirical science. It is concerned with a logical analysis of the validity of data, of which science itself is a part. Science, however, is to be investigated not as a concrete product of a particular culture within a historical situation, but rather according to its validity, that is, insofar as it is "science" in an ideal sense. Logical analysis, as advocated by Husserl, is strictly speaking "normative"—which is not to say that it is more a question of norms than of facts. It is rather a question of discovering logical rules that decide whether something may be called "science" or "a method" or "rational." Thus "reason," for example, is not given as such, either empirical or metaphysical; it acquires its meaning only in terms of logic. In a later work Husserl speaks of his phenomenology in this respect as the "self-interpretation of pure reason."

This logical and methodological approach—now championed by various philosophers but advocated by Husserl as early as 1900—can be further illustrated by the concept of space. By "space" we may understand in the first place that ordered form of the phenomenal world that is familiar to us in ordinary experience. This (factual) space-structure, however, is not the field with which geometry is concerned. When, as sometimes happens, it is thought that it *is*, mathematics, according to Husserl, gets one into a metaphysical fog, a kind of mysticism. One must view mathematics as a series of regularly interrelated objects of thought. Thus different kinds of space can by variation in the curvature and according to definite rules merge into one another. That is to say that logical rules are formulated concerning (spatial) sets, rules which enable one to determine what "space" is to mean within a given system. Husserl calls this the categorical space-form of the phenomenal world. This then leads to a whole series of formal deductive systems, since the scheme in question is logically ordered and allows for the possibility of many other systems in so far as they appear to accord *a priori* with the systems already established. Thus there may arise a series of logically interrelated geometrics—issuing not from empirical observation but from a logical act, a logical intentionality—which bring to light the coherence of rules. In his later development Husserl points out that space thus categorically conceived can be arrived at from space as empirically given by means of a certain process of "idealization."

The relation between the factual and the logical, implied in this particular process, appears in fact in his earlier work. In the first volume of his LOGICAL INVESTIGATIONS he speaks about "ideation," by which he refers to the human capacity for grasping the universal in the individual, the concept in the empirical representation. There is a conceptual intention which enables one to grasp in a number of various representations, repeated over a period of time, the identity of a logical rule—to recognize the same mathematical equation in a variety of perceptions. One can in this way become convinced—in the logical, not the psychological sense—of certain necessary rules which are independent of factual processes of thought and of empirical verification. Husserl speaks here of "ideal truths" and "truths in themselves," and so pays homage to the work of Leibniz, with his concepts of *vérités de raison* and of *mathesis universalis*, and to the work of Bolzano, with his *Sätze an sich* (rules in themselves).

That man can discover the universal and logically necessary by means of the individual and factually given carries with it the implication that logical laws can be applied to factual phenomena. Logic may, in the process, be greatly enlarged. Husserl refers to the significance of Leibniz' work and in particular to his scheme for a logic of probability, to embrace a far wider field than was the concern of traditional logic. The relation between logical rules and empirical data thus renders possible the application of logical truths, but it doesn't guarantee its validity. For the possibilities of application are unlimited. Husserl emphasizes in some separate studies on non-Euclidean geometry how the categorical (that is, non-empirical) rules disclose an ever-widening field, reaching far beyond the world of facts. When Husserl later developed his so-called phenomenological reduction, the disclosure of a non-empirical, non-factual world became the central theme of his philosophy.

The foregoing needs to be amplified at two points. First, Husserl views this grasping of the universal and logical as the "intuition" of logical essences. He doesn't mean a mystical or psychological intuition, for he explicitly rejects both of these. His use of the term "intuition" (*Anschauung, Schau, schauende Erkenntnis*) can be historically explained by the influence of Brentano's empiricism. Brentano tried to combine empirical sensation with the rationalistic idea of eternal truths. For Husserl, however, "intuition" is much wider than sensory perception; it stresses the necessity that something must be given and accepted in order to arrive at real knowledge. He wishes to make clear that even the logical act contains a representation, a given intuition of essences. This may be summarized by saying that Husserl stresses both the constructive aspects ("rules," "a deductive system," "an intentional act") and the aspect that is logically given ("intuition," *Sätze an sich*) in regard to what is logically evident.

Second—and this point is connected with the first—the word "logical" must be taken in the broadest sense: it encompasses more than logic in the ordinary sense, more too than the logic of probability and mathematics; it is intended to refer to every evident truth or evident datum that is independent of the empirical world. Even in the data of sensory perception something may present itself in its many variations as identical and so be the object of "ideation." Husserl gives the example of perceiving the color red. One may not conceive red as a substance, for it is a property of a concrete object and not, for instance, a metaphysical "part" of such an object. The red is given with the individual thing by which it is distinguished, and with that thing it also perishes. If, while observing red in an object, however, one should say: "Red is a color," one would no longer be talking about "red" as an empirical property, but about what Husserl calls "red" as a species—one might also say "red" as a structure, as a rule, in terms of which it is meaningful to speak of "red" in many (empirically) various cases, i.e., cases of objects with different shades and gradations of red. If, even in this sense, it is no metaphysical entity, still less is it simply a name used arbitrarily for a number of phenomena. It rather indicates a rule for the use of the word "red"; it is a specific meaning which doesn't depend on empirical things and about which it would be nonsense to say that this meaning would perish with the thing that is red. Here again Husserl speaks of "ideation," because "red" in this sense can be distinguished by directing one's attention to something that is red and by way of this empirical perception to "red" as a rule. Husserl speaks of this direction of mind also in terms of the verb *meinen,* in the older sense of this German word, viz., to fix attention on something. This concept of "ideation" is elaborated in Husserl's later work IDEAS, vol. I, where he distinguishes between looking at the individual existent, the fact, and looking at the essence, the *eidos.*

As we have already noted, Husserl considers the logical evidence of a statement related to the empirical world to be incontestable, because it touches the statement's meaning without regard for whether it is actually true or false—the palm-trees that prove a mirage. Pure essence, discovered by way of "ideation," has as such no effect on the facts of the case. It is evident, nonetheless, that for Husserl the logical and the factual are closely related, so that empirical data can form stepping stones for the direction of the mind to the logical and ideal. Throughout the development of Husserl's thought this connection of the logical with the factual, or as Husserl puts it later, of meaning with fact, embodies a tension. This already finds expression at the point of the *Wesensschau,* the intuition of essential features, which requires that empirical data be reduced, brought back, so to speak, to the non-empirical validity as it presents itself in them—this he calls the "eidetic reduction." The essential and timeless is, as it were, lifted out of the factual and temporal by means of intuition.

This comes under special review in the discussion of natural laws.

These, of course, cannot be known *a priori* in view of their ties with empirical facts; they are not, to sure, merely laws about facts, but they do imply the existence of facts. These considerations appear to be in conflict with his now notorious remark about the gravitation law of Newton, a remark which has been heavily attacked as extremist. Husserl says that the law of gravitation existed before Newton discovered it and that even if every gravitating mass were annihilated the law itself would not thereby be abrogated. Is then a natural law, which—unlike the laws of logic—is tied up directly with matters of fact, not in this way hypostasized to a kind of Platonic, trans-empirical reality?

These problems can be solved if one views these statements in the context of Husserl's other explanations of natural law. A natural law can only be justified in terms of the facts of empirical observation. That is to say, one can arrive at such a law by way of induction. However, an essential distinction must be made here. Induction does not of itself ensure that the natural law is valid; it ensures only that its validity is more or less probable. It is the aim of the natural sciences to formulate this validity exactly and thereby to loosen the ties with the world of facts. In this sense the exact formulation of the law of gravitation would not be what has actually been formulated by astronomy; it would take on rather a form like the following: on the basis of our present-day knowledge and in terms of the experience available to our present resources it is theoretically sound to affirm that the formulation of Newton—and any other mathematical rule that can be related to it—is very probably valid. Husserl wrote this in about 1900, long before the formulation of the general law of relativity, which is in a certain sense, however, contained as a logical possibility in Husserl's formulation.

The laws established by the exact sciences about questions of fact are "authentic laws," but from a methodological and epistemological point of view they are "idealizing fictions," according to Husserl, though fictions *cum fundamento in re*. An exact formulation of the law of gravitation must be distinguished from statements about the probability with which this law may be applied to factual situations. The law as such tells us nothing about the existence of gravitating mass, but it gives us a logical rule for deciding what is to be understood by "gravitating mass."

Thus Husserl drafted an ambitious and comprehensive program for a logical investigation that was to penetrate the empirical and factual world so as ultimately to leave it behind in the discovery of "eternal" and evident validity. By "eternal"—Husserl himself put it often in quotation-marks—he meant that this validity cannot be affected by the changes in the world of facts and so stands apart from human history.

Brief Bibliography

O. Becker, "Beiträge zur phänomenologischen Begrundung der Geometrie," *Jahrbuch f. philos. und phänomen. Forschung*, vol. 6(1923).

Marvin Farber, *The Foundation of Phenomenology*, Cambridge, Mass., 1943.

H. Fels, "Bolzano und Husserl," *Philos. Jahrbuch der Görresgesellschaft*, 1926.

I. Fisch, *Husserls Intentionalitäts- und Urteilslehre*, Basel, 1942.

E. Husserl, *Logische Untersuchungen*, I and II (3 vols.), Halle a.S., 1900, 1901 (revised ed., 1913, 1921).

———, "Philosophy as Rigorous Science," tr. by Q. Lauer, *Cross Currents*, vol. 6(1956), pp. 227-246, 325-344.

———, "Phenomenology," *The Encyclopedia Britannica*, 14th ed., vol. 17, London, 1929. Better text in original German in *Phänomenologische Psychologie*, The Hague, 1962.

E. Levinas, *La théorie de l'intuition dans la phénoménologie de Husserl*, Paris, 1930.

P. Natorp, "Zur Frage nach der logische Methode; mit Bezug auf E. Husserls 'Prolegomena zur einen Logik,'" *Kantstudien*, vol. 6(1901).

A. Osborn, *The Philosophy of Edmund Husserl and His Logical Investigations*, Cambridge, Mass., 1949 (1st ed., New York, 1934).

M. Palàgy, *Der Streit der Psychologisten und Formalisten in der modernen Logik*, Leipzig, 1902.

R. Schérer, *La phénoménologie des "Recherches logiques" de Husserl*, Paris, 1967.

H. Spiegelberg, *The Phenomenological Movement*, 2 vols., 2nd ed., The Hague, 1965.

K. Twardowski, *Zur Lehre vom Inhalt und Gegenstand der Vorstellungen*, Vienna, 1894.

J. Wilming, *Husserls Lehre von den intentionalen Erlebnissen*, Leipzig, 1925.

Chapter Three

Phenomenological Reduction and Factual Existence

THE "phenomenological reduction" forms a dominant theme in the philosophy of Husserl. While it is not our purpose to sketch the whole development of Husserl's thought, it needs to be pointed out that this theme, like a number of others, was not to be found in his system from the very beginning. Phenomenology as originally viewed by Husserl was a method. Only later did it grow into a comprehensive philosophy in which the phenomenological reduction was to play an important role. By means of this reduction the validity of reality is left out of account for the purpose of achieving a more comprehensive and fundamental investigation of logical structures, which contain empirical reality as simply one of the valid possibilities within the wider, purely phenomenological field.

Perhaps the best way to clarify all this is to trace the first intimations of the phenomenological reduction in Husserl's thought before he began to speak of it in these strictly methodological terms. We may refer first of all to the mathematical habit of mind that time and again reveals itself in Husserl. We have noted already his clear distinction between empirical space and conceptual space, as this is employed in mathematics in direct relation to logical operations. The logical categories appear to disclose an area far more extensive than empirical experience, which is concerned with what is actually given in reality.

If we pursue this line of procedure, we come to the "eidetic reduction," discussed in the preceding chapter. What is given empirically is then analyzed logically and structurally, that is to say, in terms of what is essential to it, its *eidos,* which can be intuited quite apart from the senses. Husserl deliberately used the term *eidos* to replace the words "idea" and "ideal" which he had used previously and which had given rise to misunderstandings. He did not want to indicate a transempirical, ideal reality but to indicate and analyze the essence (*eidos*) of certain aspects of the given reality. A modern translation of *eidos*, then, would be essential structure. The way in which Husserl described the method of classical physics, by reference to Newton's law of gravitation, was actually an illustration of this "intuiting of essences" (*Wesens-schau*), since the formulation of this law, viewed as the most probable estimate at a particular period of time, no longer related to the actual existence of gravitating mass, but to its logical essence, to what we are to take "gravitating mass" to mean.

The tendency now arises to withdraw phenomenological investigation from that which is empirically and factually given. It is evident too that the phenomenological method as a logical investigation is not cut loose from facts, but takes them as its point of departure. In the later developments of phenomenology, to be discussed in Chapter Seven, the question of fact is taken up in a quite new way so that it leads to new kinds of tension. Until then, however, the effect of the phenomenological reduction is precisely to eliminate the world of facts.

Husserl's expositions of what he calls "pure grammar" move in the same direction (see the second volume of his LOGICAL INVESTIGATIONS), and link up with his views on the analysis of a concept like "gravitating mass" apart from the question of its actual existence. We should here point out the distinction that Husserl makes, almost incidentally, between various uses of language, a distinction that has gained much attention in the tradition of empiricism, positivism and linguistic analysis. Language is not merely descriptive or analytical. In ordinary usage it takes on various forms, as for example in statements like, "I wonder whether . . . ," "I order you to . . . ," etc. Language that gives expression to command is to be sharply distinguished from the language of description, because it cannot be asked whether the content of such a sentence is true or false. Husserl does not maintain that the question of truth is not to be applied, but that truth in this case coincides with the truthfulness of the speaker. Husserl speaks of expressions of this kind as subjective statements and distinguishes them from statements relating to something objective, where it is possible therefore to ask the material question of what they might mean.

The investigation of meaning is the so-called "pure grammar." It has to be distinguished from questions about the truth or falsity of statements. It is concerned, nonetheless, with propositions in the narrower sense, with those, namely, where the question of objective truth or falsity may properly be posed. This is possible, however, only if the content of a sentence is meaningful irrespective of whether it is true or false. The forms of meaning that are to be discovered have as their criterion that they draw the line between sense (*Sinn*) and nonsense (*Unsinn*). An accumulation of words that are meaningful in themselves can yield sheer nonsense; e.g., "king but or similar and." There are therefore certain rules or laws that make meaningful statements or groupings of words. Two levels can be distinguished here. To ask whether something is true or false is to require, first of all, a logical investigation into its material meaning, that is, its meaning with regard to the possibility or impossibility of the states of affairs referred to—and this, of course, in the logical sense and not, for example, in the physical sense. "The tree is purple" is meaningful *qua* logical meaning, even though it refers to what is physically impossible. "Number is purple" and "the circle is square" are altogether excluded by such an analysis from the sphere of what is meaningful in the material sense. Husserl doesn't call these examples "meaningless" but "absurd," that is to say, contrary to meaning.

This contradiction is to be understood as material, and Husserl speaks therefore of a "synthetic" contradiction. He does this in order to distinguish it from a higher logical level. On this higher level purely analytical laws hold, since the "material" is here disregarded and only "formal" logical relations are held in view. The lower level is subordinate to the higher; it must in a logical respect concur with it, but not *vice versa*. For in purely logical analysis, in terms of sense and nonsense, considerations of material possibilities—of whether an utterance is true or false, or even of whether it runs counter to meaning—have to be set aside. Husserl refers to this higher level as "apophantic logic," and on it propositions like "the tree is purple" and "number is green" are all meaningful. The meaning of such statements may be complete, even though, from a factual point of view, they are about impossibilities. Formally speaking, sentences like "more intensive is round" and "the house is equal" are analytically impossible, formally meaningless, since the logical rules have been broken. In investigations like these Husserl clearly had in view, as he himself remarked, a kind of *mathesis universalis,* such as Leibniz had hoped to attain.

Husserl was still occupied with these questions in 1929 when he published his *Formal and Transcendental Logic* in which he elaborated his ideas on pure logic. He compares his apophantic analysis with that of Aristotle, where propositions of a form such as "S is P" (cf. "the tree is purple," "the circle is square") consist of variable terms. Yet this formal, classical logic lies so far behind the symbolic logic of our own time as well as what Husserl himself has in mind that Aristotle persistently relates his analysis to the real world and thus does not exclude from it the categories of reality; his analysis is still not entirely formal. Husserl here points out the importance of logical operations and especially—as the most characteristic of pure analysis—the principle of noncontradictory logic: one has to define noncontradiction, that is, the laws which regulate what may and what may not be analytically implied.

In an appendix Husserl himself connected the apophantic analysis with the concept of tautology as that had been developed in recent logic. For knowledge, according to Husserl, was not being enriched, but being analyzed as it is—though for such a "clarification" one often needs the genius of a mathematician. Husserl here inserts a note of O. Becker's which connects this analysis with the analysis given by Wittgenstein in his *Tractatus,* especially in terms of the concept of tautology.

To what has been written so far a new aspect has to be added, which will again bring to the fore the difference between Husserl's ideas and those of logical empiricism. The purpose of his logical investigations is not simply to produce an inventory of logical rules or laws, but also to define the objectifying acts in which alone these rules can become manifest. One may here recall what was said in the previous chapter about the specific activity of consciousness, "apperception," as the condition for identifying things in a number of different acts (*e.g.*, identifying one mathematical equation in many acts of memory and observation). This correlation of logical objectivity and the activity of the subject is, in a certain sense, already present in Husserl's pre-phenomenological work and especially in his PHILOSOPHY OF ARITHMETIC. But there the activity of consciousness was still described very much in psychological terms. He abandoned this idea in the first volume of his LOGICAL INVESTIGATIONS partly under the influence of Frege. In the second volume of the work, however, he re-focussed his attention on the activity of consciousness, but now in the logical sense. (The new idea was not altogether absent in the first volume: witness his concept of "evidence.") The consequence, however, was that outsiders looked upon Husserl's views as a piece of psychological research, although, as it should by now have become clear, his concern was precisely with logical analysis. More relevant, however, is the question of Husserl's "idealism." Many of his own disciples, on noticing him move toward a certain idealism, a "transcendental idealism" as he himself called it at a later stage, went their own ways, whereas originally they had interpreted his analyses as a move toward realism, a return to "the things themselves." In order properly to understand these tensions, one must bear in mind that Husserl's attempt to analyze the logical apart from any dependence on factual states of affairs led naturally to his phenomenological reduction, with its attempt to eliminate empirical reality. Further, that this phenomenological reduction fixed attention the more firmly on the activity of consciousness. Both these points will be further discussed in what follows.

In his LOGICAL INVESTIGATIONS he gives a description of logical laws in relation to consciousness as intentional experience, that is to say, consciousness viewed not as a psychological datum, but in terms of its logical nature as being-directed-towards. Already in 1907 Husserl showed himself to be dissatisfied with this. This phenomenology, he said, was merely descriptive psychology and as such it was far too closely bound up with what was naturally and empirically given. It was in order to sift out these latter elements that he took up the phenomenological reduction. This stands at the center of his second major work, IDEAS. INTRODUCTION TO PURE PHENOMENOLOGY (English ed. of Volume One, London, 1931), where his idealistic tendencies first came to the notice of his readers. But as early as 1907 he had expounded his phenomenological reduction in lectures, which were published only after his death, in 1950, under the title IDEA OF PHENOMENOLOGY (English ed., 1964, The Hague).

The phenomenological reduction is, methodologically considered, an attempt to set aside every kind of "natural," empirically derived, knowledge. Its purpose is to open up a new dimension of investigation, related to the older dimensions, it is true—the image of "dimension" implies this, as Husserl himself points out—but which is still to be contrasted as such to those of the natural world. To this world belongs *inter alia* the natural validity of everything given. And to this attitude, which Husserl also speaks of as "mundaneness," belongs not only so-called naive experience, but also psychology, physics and even mathematics. In his IDEAS he maintains further that the phenomenological attitude is not to be acquired by easy transition from the natural or mundane attitude. This might well be so for the transition from ordinary perception to eidetic intuition, and for the transition from empirical to geometric space. For here it is only a question of modifying the ordinary attitude which people assume toward their environment.

To bring about the phenomenological reduction one has to eliminate the question of reality as such. That is to say, one has to suspend judgment about reality—perform the so-called *epoché* —by bracketing what is actual or real in phenomena (a tree observed, an event remembered, one psychological life, etc.). It is clear from the idea of "bracketing" that all this doesn't in the least deny the existence of reality, as is done by some forms of scepticism, nor even the reality of the outside world, as is done by some forms of idealism. It means, according to Husserl, not dissolving the world, but receiving it, assimilating it, by means of bracketing it in a dimension of absolute validity. This will become clearer by noting that the phenomenological reduction is metaphysically unpretentious and that, factually speaking, it neither adds to nor subtracts from reality, but puts the very claim to existence out of court. This is more, then, of a logical procedure for clearing one's view of a more fundamental validity.

Husserl maintains, in a statement that has become well known, that if one should take "positivism" to mean the absolute, unprejudiced foundation of the sciences on the positive, that is, on what is directly and originally grasped, then phenomenology can be said to propagate the true positivism. In the phenomenological reduction one is no longer concerned about what may or may not exist, but about the structure of the phenomena as such. One has to analyze how they present themselves, how they become defined in consciousness. What lies behind the phenomena is no longer of interest; what is important is how they behave in the purely logical field, how they present themselves "immanently."

Two points need to be added here to clear away any possible misunderstanding. Someone could ask whether this phenomenological reduction, with its deliberate disregard of everything real, does not carry one into an imaginary world. Can one in this way distinguish between, say, a perception and an hallucination? Can one still keep imagination and memory apart? It is not, however, the intention of the phenomenological method to wipe out such distinctions; it is precisely to sharpen their profile. This is not to say that it allows metaphysical discussion on the question of whether an authentic world is to be found behind our perceptions, or whether perception is essentially different from imagination. But the boundary is maintained between the directly given phenomenon that we call perception and the phenomenon to be logically classified as hallucination. This is possible only by refusing to speculate about phenomena, by conceiving them as they are presented. Within this methodological perspective, references to what lies beyond them—positively, in perception; negatively, in hallucination—then belong to the structure of the phenomenon itself, to the logical rules which, when analyzed, justify one in speaking in the one case of "perception," and in the other of "hallucination." Instead of the difference between perception and hallucination, memory and imagination, and so forth, being wiped out, they are made the more apparent, because the metaphysical question of a reality behind phenomena is replaced by the logical question of the meaning of such phenomena. This meaning is partly determined by the positive or negative claim to reality that such phenomena might make.

A second question, a little further in the same direction, concerns the words "immanent" and "consciousness." These words are used to denote the field of absolute validity, made accessible by the process of bracketing "reality." Is this then to say that reality is retracted and subsumed under the immanent sphere of human, or possibly absolute, consciousness? By no means; phenomenology has no use for such metaphysical concepts. This becomes clear when we observe that the phenomenological reduction is a suspension of judgment, not only concerning the reality of the world around us, but also concerning the reality of man himself. Although Husserl shows a growing interest in the thought of Descartes and in the methodic doubt which led to the *cogito*, he always laid stress on the difference between Descartes and himself. For the phenomenological reduction, while being itself methodical and so having much to learn from philosophical doubt, is in no sense a form of erosive doubt. No, the real world is left untouched; it is even viewed, in terms of its logical validity, as within an absolute dimension. A further point of difference, worked out by Husserl in his CARTESIAN MEDITATIONS, is that Descartes stopped at the point of his own consciousness (*cogito*). The world, fellowmen, God and even the truths of science are doubted, but not his own consciousness. Husserl, on the other hand, brackets reality as a whole, including that of the empirical "I" and of factual consciousness, so as to be able to take out of brackets the structure and logical pretentions of all phenomena.

Here, in principle, is an answer to the second question. Husserl, like Kant to whose work he gave more and more attention, calls his method transcendental. This differs to such a degree from the more empirical method of the LOGICAL INVESTIGATIONS that it eliminates everything empirical, empirical consciousness included, so as to lay open to view the structural conditions. This concern with

conditions is what gives it the name "transcendental" in the
Kantian sense. The phenomenological reduction, then, is also a
transcendental method, which is not to say that it means a with-
drawal into the psychologically immanent, by proceeding, for
example, as if the observed tree did not actually exist; it means
rather a reaching out to what in all phenomena is logically evident.
Husserl here refers to the comparison that is sometimes made
between empirical consciousness and a box containing various
states of consciousness that are relative to an outer world. Husserl
emphatically rejects such comparisons. When he speaks of "immanence" he has in mind the structure of phenomena, with a view
to tracing the rules that decide how we may speak meaningfully
about objects of observation, of hallucination, of memory, and so
forth.

One can find illustrations of this method throughout his work.
We must mention in particular a work which is of great significance
for the whole of Husserl's development, his lectures on time consciousness given between 1905 and 1910, and published in 1928
as THE PHENOMENOLOGY OF INTERNAL TIME-CONSCIOUSNESS (English
ed., Bloomington, Ind., 1964). He analyzes here the way in which
an enduring object is identified in the succession of time and on
the basis of observations separated in time. The object is not
multiplied according to the number of observations, but remains
one and the same throughout. What rules can be said to have been
obeyed in the discernment of an object? When is the identity
broken? What is the meaning of the word "now," that is to say,
what rules can be said to control its use, as for example, when one
says "I can now hear a flute," where the "now" is certainly not
limited to the fraction of a moment, but possesses a certain dura-
bility in time? It is questions like these that are posed within the
"immanence" of purely logical and phenomenological analysis of
meaning. Elsewhere Husserl writes that to investigate the phenomenon "thing"—the observed or remembered thing, its place in
time, its relation to the wider thing-world, etc.—is not to ask for
a metaphysical view of the substance of the thing. Is it purely
material? purely spiritual, a combination of percepts or sense-
data? Within the phenomenological reduction the "thing," viewed

not as a bit of "reality," but as a certain structure, proves to be definable in terms of a series of "rules."

It is worth making clear at this point that these analyses are to be viewed in dynamic terms. The "rules" here are something quite other than established laws, to be found "out there" in the objective world—it is precisely this that is bracketed. No, these rules are *at work* and so become visible. Even in his early work, as appeared in the previous chapter, Husserl speaks of the activity by which alone something can show itself identical in a multiplicity of momentary phenomena. This "apperception," as the activity of consciousness by which something is conceived as this or that, as unity or diversity, as real or as unreal, as dependent or as independent (as a property, for example), proves to be essential for the manifestation of the rules which govern these meanings.

In other words, the dynamics of the rules is given together with the activity of consciousness. "Consciousness" here is in no respect to be equated with empirical consciousness, for the scope of the phenomenological reduction is the transcendental, not the factual, the logical, not the psychological. Man himself, his empirical "I," his actual consciousness, all these are part of the time-space world. And this natural world is bracketed so as to make room for an investigation of the rules that govern its meanings. These rules, as we have observed, do not rest upon the reality at our disposal; they "take place" and so form, as it were, a dynamic field of self-constitutive meanings ("thing," "tree," "time," "perception," "hallucination," "real," "apparent," "number," "physical law," etc.). This field, this activity by which something is conceived as this or that, is "consciousness" in the logical, non-empirical, non-metaphysical sense. All meanings, and thus the entire natural world, including the empirical consciousness, are reflected in this logical process. Husserl likes to formulate it as follows: meanings are constituted in the pure consciousness, which is thus a stream of logically analyzable experience. Reality as a whole, when analyzed, appears as purely intentional being, that is to say, as relative, not metaphysical being, being that displays itself to "consciousness."

These ideas culminate in difficult formulations which appear at first glance to be sheer metaphysical idealism, but which in fact abandon entirely any speculation about "reality" or "being," and discuss these concepts only to analyze their meaning. Within phenomenological research, Husserl states, expressions like "absolute reality" and "absolute being" are contradictions in terms. For the research is concerned to arrive at their meaning; these words must fall back on something else, and so cannot be absolute—but fall back on what? On their "sense," that is, on consciousness as a logical field where meanings are constituted. The word "absolute," therefore, is never applicable to something real, only to a validity that cannot be further reduced. That's why Husserl can write that this immanent, logical field, this non-empirical consciousness is "absolute" because in principle it "needs no other 'matter' for its own existence"—which is the classical formula, used, e.g., by Descartes and Spinoza, to describe metaphysically the concept of substance.

Summarizing Husserl's various rather complicated explanations, referred to in the preceding paragraphs, his position about the content of the word "meaning"—which is the classical problems about the status of univerals—may be characterized as follows. Husserl's attempt to discern the "logical essence" of a phenomenon amounts to the analysis of the meaning of a concept. This meaning cannot be defined by the factual usage—by psychological or social conventions—but by the sense the concept necessarily has when one discerns "meaning" (*Bedeutung*) as something which, on the one hand, is directly given and, on the other, never confined to the structures of temporal reality. Both these aspects point to Husserl's twofold position with respect to the traditional conceptions about the status of universals in the following way.

On the one hand, unlike Plato, he doesn't localize universals in a special, higher realm of reality. He doesn't, in this sense, separate "meaning" (essence) from daily reality (existence); therefore, his analysis of meaning is closer to that of empiricists, logical positivists and analytical philosophers who describe logical meaning as a prescription for the usage of a word.

On the other hand, Husserl makes a more logically defined separation between "meaning" and factual reality, in the sense that the logical structure of a meaning can be regarded (even "intuited") as something given in itself (*eidos*) which is not temporal. For example, Pythagoras' proposition has a kind of logical "existence" even if we have forgotten its proof, even if Pythagoras would never have discovered it, and even if mankind would no longer exist. Husserl differs here from a more empiricist and positivistic approach, which would relate such a logical validity to a community of philosophers and scientists who accept the validity of such rules in a given period of history. But doesn't a logical essence or rule require a consciousness? Such a question arising from a more idealistic line of thought Husserl would, indeed, answer in the affirmative, but only if one defines "consciousness" neither psychologically (as the consciousness of an individual man) nor metaphysically (as a higher, superhuman consciousness existing in itself, such as Hegel's *Geist*), but in a transcendental way. The term "transcendental" indicates here the purely logical aspect of all real processes in which "meanings" disclose themselves.

Husserl's doctrine thus developed into a philosophy of his own, which can well be called "transcendental idealism" and in which the logical and anti-metaphysical structure of things occupies the center.

Brief Bibliography

G. Berger, *Le cogito dans la Philosophie de Husserl*, Paris, 1941.

E. Fink, "Die phänomenologische Philosophie E. Husserls in der gegenwärtigen Kritik," *Kantstudien*, vol. 37(1933). Also contained in Fink's *Studien zur Phänomenologie* (*1930-1939*), The Hague, 1966.

E. Husserl, *The Idea of Phenomenology*, tr. by W. P. Alson and G. Nakhnikian, The Hague, 1964.

———, *Ideas*, tr. by W. R. Boyce-Gibson, New York, 1931.

————, *The Phenomenology of Internal Time-consciousness,* tr. by J. C. Churchill; introduction by C. O. Schrag, The Hague, 1964.

Q. Lauer, *Phénoménologie de Husserl. Essai sur la genèse de l'intentionnalité,* Paris, 1954.

A. de Muralt, *L'idée de la phénoménologie,* Paris, 1958.

Th. Seebohm, *Die Bedingungen der Möglichkeit der Transzendental-Philosophie,* Bonn, 1962.

W. Szilasi, *Einführung in die Phenomenologie Husserls,* The Hague, 1964.

H. Van Breda, "La Réduction phénoménologique," *Husserl* (*Cahiers de Royaumont*), Paris, 1959.

A. de Waelhens, *Phénoménologie et Vérité,* Paris, 1953.

Chapter Four

Logical Positivism and the Problem of Meaning

As MUCH as two hundred years ago British empiricists, like Hume and Locke, had given a logical analysis of human knowledge, to be followed later by the positivists. Their results, however, bore a strong psychological color, and not until we come to the school of Vienna do we find the attempt at a strict separation of the logical and the psychological analyses of knowledge. This led to a new insight into the nature and use of analytical propositions, where the proposition was found to disclose what was already implied in the concepts, axioms and rules employed, which led in turn to a new description of tautology, as will be further explained in what follows. With this logically purer insight into analytical propositions they were the better able to mark out the field of non-analytical, synthetic propositions, that is, propositions that furnish new information, being related to factual data.

This becomes more comprehensible if we keep in mind that the intention of the logical positivist thinkers was to divorce logic or the doctrine of propositions from the sphere of sense-perception. Traditional logic made the distinction between the connotation (*intensio*) and denotation (*extensio*) of a concept, in the sense that in proportion as the first was greater the second was lesser, and *vice versa*. In more psychological terms: the more instances that a concept encompassed, the less one was able to conceive the connotation of such a concept (compare, for example, the following series: fox-terrier, dog, mammal, vertebrate, living being, being). In the development of the new logic Frege has presented a project for giving logic a better hold, as it were, on the content of a concept (by means of the so-called *Satzfunktion*). The discovery of certain antinomies in the logic of classes, connected with the impossibility in certain cases of indicating the denotation of a concept (*e.g.*, the concept of "odd number"), urged the setting up of certain logical conditions that could be regarded as a definition of a class. Then "x ∈ M" (x is an element of class M) would mean: "x fulfills the following conditions. . . ." It was Bertrand Russell who developed this logic of classes, continuing in this respect the researches of Frege. As with the sensory element, so now the psychological element was eliminated from logic. The perception of content was reduced to logical rules and the classes lost their character as representing the way things really are; there could then be classes that were quite empty.

With reference to this development in modern logic, Carnap urged, around 1930, that the concept of class be done away with altogether. In symbolic logic, according to Carnap, a class is not the sum of its elements, but an expression of what these elements have in common. His conclusion is that in contemporary logic the denotation has been ousted in favor of the connotation. But this has been possible only because the prevalent attitude has been against psychologism. For psychological analysis has had to give way to purely logical analysis. The first confuses the (logical) connotation of a concept with its (psychological) representation. The whole development of logical positivist thought, as advocated by Carnap and the Vienna school, is closely connected, however, with the conviction that where a representation is lacking there is by no means necessarily a lack of conceptual content. The peculiar, autonomous value of conceptual distinction, independent of, and sometimes even contrary to, perceptibility, will prove to be of import for other themes developed in this book.

A logical determination of the connotation of a concept requires an investigation into the rules according to which a concept functions. The fabric of these rules is called logical grammar. Its construction was begun by, among others, Carnap and Schlick, in about 1920, though the work of Wittgenstein at that time needs also to be mentioned. Carnap spoke of "logical syntax," a term which he fully expounded in a book of that name.

By logical syntax we are to understand the philosophico-logical investigation of statements, rather than of objects. It comprises, then, a set of statements about statements, not statements about things. It has, as such, no sector of reality to which it may direct itself. Zoology, for example, occupies itself with the characteristics of animals. Logical analysis, understood as a philosophical activity, directs its attention toward the logical connections of zoological statements. Whenever questions are raised in philosophy concerning objects themselves, there are two possibilities. Either they concern objects which do not belong to philosophy—objects like "man," "society," "nature," "space and time"—in which case they must be referred to the sciences, or they concern objects which cannot be investigated by the sciences, in which case they are only quasi-objects, such as traditional philosophy is full of: "being," "nothingness," "the absolute," "norms." How were these quasi-objects ever arrived at? Why do they play so great a role in the history of philosophy? Because they are essentially expressions of feeling. Men have here given expression, in the concealed form of logic, to their own desires or to their emotional reaction to the world about them.

Metaphysics and value-judgments (as discussed in traditional ethics, for example), as well as all theological statements, are thus debarred from the field of knowledge.

These ideas were strongly represented in the Vienna school; fifteen years later they had become well known through the early work of Ayer, while they gained influence abroad through the work of men like Richard von Mises, where they became closely linked with the views of Ernst Mach. Only at a much later phase, in which the posthumous works of Wittgenstein played a significant part, was this bifurcation of questions into those that were clearly philosophical and those that were not, done away with. But to this we shall return in the final chapters.

The grounds for rejecting the questions concerned lie in the fact that, on the assumptions of the Vienna school, it is impossible to establish the meaning of statements about God, beauty, the soul, ethical values and so forth. What *may* be called meaningful is analytical propositions, because these simply expound what one already has in one's conceptual apparatus and rules of operation; and further, synthetic propositions which are material in reference and not merely formal, that is to say, capable of being either true or false, which in turn depends on the actual states of affairs to which the statements purport to refer. Frege had already observed that with certain kinds of statements it was impossible to establish their logical meaning. These he called "false." Russell had distinguished, more clearly, between meaningful statements, which could be either true or false—though analytical statements were also to be included—and meaningless statements.

This division has become quite customary, almost without variation. A statement like "this painting is fine," "this deed is bad," "God exists" or "God does not exist" is neither true nor false, since it cannot be verified (or falsified), while on the other hand it is not analytical: such a statement is therefore meaningless. At best, it can be regarded as an indication of one's being aesthetically or religiously moved, or of one's trying to move someone else. In any event, it is denied the status of knowledge; it may indeed stir and stimulate, exhort and edify, but it will not impart new insight or information; nor will it, like analytical propositions, clarify knowledge we already have.

Both Carnap and Schlick made use of these distinctions. Schlick did so, to be sure, in his own peculiar way, in the interests of cultural and ethical problems, but in the event he reduced ethics to the verifiable statements of a science: psychology. Carnap, however, pointed to another treacherous use of language, to what he called "pseudo-object sentences." One must distinguish the following:

(a) object sentences, e.g., "5 is a prime number," "Babylon is a great city." These object sentences belong to the domain of the sciences.

(b) Pseudo-object sentences, e.g., "5 is not a thing, but a number," "Babylon was discussed in yesterday's lecture." Here certain terms are wrongly employed, and can be put right only by being transferred into the following group.

(c) Syntactic sentences, e.g., "'5' is not a thing-word but a number-word," " 'Babylon' as a word came up in yesterday's lecture."

Logical syntax is offered here as a means of escaping certain dangers attending linguistic usage. It concerns, in this case, the tendency to treat nouns as entities, or even as substances. The danger becomes particularly serious when concepts themselves are substantialized. Concepts are not a kind of ethereal object, but need to be reduced to the logical rules, the syntax, within which they function—compare here what was earlier said about logical classes.

The concept is nothing real. This is emphasized particularly by Schlick, who thereby distinguishes between the concept as a psychological datum and the concept in the logical sense. It cannot be denied that in concept formation all sorts of psychological factors come into play. The image, in this way, plays a significant role; but not in the logical sense, for it yields no logical certainty and represents only imperfectly the logical status of the concept. How, then, is the logical status of the concept determined, if this is independent of empirical and, especially, psychological data? By the logical function of the concept, and this consists in defining relations, co-ordinating (*zuordnen*) elements. This, in its turn, is determined by logical rules.

Important here, as with Husserl too, is the logical fixing of identities. The criterion of truth in a logical argument, as in the methodology of a particular science, is logical identity, which is to be found in all its statements. If the distinction between analytical and synthetic propositions—or, as Schlick would rather have it, the distinction between *vérités de raison* and *vérités de fait*—is to be maintained, the necessity of logical identity in both cases at once becomes obvious. In the first case, that of purely conceptual propositions, it should be evident that by means of analysis or deduction the conclusion can be shown to be already contained in the premises. In the second case we are dealing with propositions about actual states of affairs. And here we need verification, that is to say, we need to establish whether something is or is not the case. We then put our verification in the form of a proposition. But here we are liable to error: do I really see a tree, or is it hallucination? Such a proposition, therefore, needs to be amplified by a series of further propositions: that of a doctor for example, who affirms it to be highly improbable that on such and such a date I was subject to hallucination; those of other persons who also testify to having seen a tree there; that of the natural scientist who considers the appearance of a tree at that spot not altogether improbable, and so on. In principle, of course, one could extend such a series *ad infinitum,* but in practice it would not be necessary. The logical requirement is simply that in a number of statements the same logical identity should make itself apparent. This identity is thus the criterion for the truth of such a synthetic proposition.

It becomes clear from all this that the concept is nothing real in itself; it has to be seen in its logical function. Concepts, according to Schlick, consist neither in things nor in thought. Their function is to point out logical relations, but for this they need "discretion," that is, they need clearly to define the logical boundaries. It is not then surprising that Schlick also protests against psychologism, because the psychological status of a concept, its perceptible representation, for example, is lacking in this power of sharp discrimination. For the same reason Schlick protests against introducing the "feeling of evidence" as a criterion of truth. This can appear as a psychological accompaniment, as when, for example, one "knows it is right." But precisely because the feeling here is psychological, it is lacking in the power of logical discrimination. This is evident from the fact that one can be so easily mistaken about one's feeling. A classical blunder is the *quarternio terminorum,* which argues that in a syllogism four terms may be used, instead of the three allowed, because one concept is employed in a twofold sense. The logical "discretion" of the concept is lost.

The same has been said, though even more pointedly, by Wittgenstein, both in his TRACTATUS and the dispersed memoranda that were brought together in his NOTEBOOKS (1914-1916). Russell had spoken of self-evidence as playing a part in the discernment of the rules of logic. This Wittgenstein rejected, because a genuine logic by its very structure prevented logical blunders being made; "logic must take care of itself." Schlick is aware of the views of Husserl and, while repudiating the "feeling of evidence" as a logical argument, he rejects these views. The central issue is how logical analyses are to be disentangled from psychological processes and given a meaning of their own. Husserl's view is this: by means of evidence. But is this any more than a subjective, psychological conception? He viewed this evidence, however, not as a psychological datum—for him too the psychological sense of evidence is only an attendant phenomenon—but as that quality of a proposition from which it can be known to be a true proposition. Schlick maintains, on the other hand, that evidence may refer to erroneous propositions. He considers the tendency in Husserl to speak of truth as a logical feature of propositions to be at fault. Truth is to be found only in the relation of one proposition to others and, as regards propositions concerning reality, in attaching (in logical identity through a series of propositions) certain characteristics to a state of affairs.

Schlick throws light on the distinction between what is factual and empirical, on the one hand, and what is logical, on the other, by the example of a calculating-machine. Just as with the process of thought the logical and psychological are given together but need as such to be sharply distinguished, so too the physical and mathematical aspects have to be distinguished in a calculating-machine. Viewed purely physically, a calculating-machine never works perfectly, but the result of these physico-mechanical operations is nevertheless entirely accurate. This comes about because two operations are given in one, one running continuously, the other discretely. One can introduce discrete distinctions even in continuous processes. It is thus possible to mark out the mathematical boundaries in physical data, as is done, for example, in astronomy. The calculating-machine may, in this respect, be compared to the human psyche. The psychological processes of human thought are never logically discrete as such, but they may well register logically pure distinctions. The essential feature of concepts, therefore, is not their psychological quality, their perceptible content for instance, but the moment of discretion, and thus the logical quality which this brings to light.

The distinction between the factual and the logical is here, as with Husserl, illustrated further by the concept of space. Many thinkers of the Vienna school go into great detail here. The distinction is made, with variations in terminology, between "perceptible space" and "categorical space." The first, according to Carnap, is the basis of physical space, the second of axiomatic space. Schlick refers to the work of D. Hilbert in mathematics. An axiom, for him, is not based on perceptibility, as if, in thinking of a "point," one had to imagine a grain of sand, or, in thinking of "straight," a line. No, axioms have here become purely categorical, that is, non-perceptible: they are implicit definitions. Terms such as "point" and "straight" mean purely and simply what is established in the axioms concerned. Concepts have a merely logical-discrete (not perceptible) function. So the term "plane" can mean the same in the geometry of Riemann as in the spherical geometry of Euclid.

The significance of this is that geometry is detached from the empirically given. Geometric "space" can no more be derived from physical space than the concept of "justice" can be derived from certain psychological events, such as feelings. It is still possible, of course, to bring geometric concepts to bear on what is given in perception, but then strict precision can no longer be guaranteed. Of itself the geometric concept of space is a conceptual construction and so allows for the possibility of far more extensive operations (as Husserl has already maintained), so that one can even raise the question of whether it should still be called "space." Carnap distinguishes axiomatic geometry with its implicit definitions of "point," "straight," "plane," "intersection," "between" etc. from physical, applied geometry, where a physical length is called "l" if this is congruent with the standard gage in Paris, or where a beam of light in a vacuum is taken to be a "straight line."

The foregoing can be stated as follows: knowledge in the logical, non-psychological sense is not the kind of knowledge that depends on empirical data. This knowledge is not then directed towards the existence of anything; it is knowing not *that* something is, but *"as what"* it is conceived or known. And here lies the point of

departure for the logical positivist critique of Husserl. Schlick
blames Husserl for conceiving logical knowledge in such a way
that it is, notwithstanding, knowledge of something. It is still here
a question of "perception," even though Husserl wants to speak
of a non-sensory perception that is directed toward the universal
("essence") as being something beside and beyond the individual
that has to be observed by the senses. Husserl, in other words,
attributes to the logical concept a reality of its own, which leads
him into talk about "ideal essences," "rules existing in themselves"
(*Sätze as sich*). There are no concepts, however, that actually
exist in reality or thought, for a "concept" is the function of indicating logical relations and logical discretion. The "meanings"
brought to light by logical investigation must not, therefore, be
substantialized, or we shall find ourselves once again in the mists
of metaphysical speculation.

The question of whether "meanings" do or do not exist became
a subject for debate in about 1900, even among the logical positivists. Husserl had spoken of the peculiar status of meanings,
which was not to be classed with the physical or psychological
orders of reality. And in this he was not alone. Bolzano, in a
certain sense, had preceded him here. Frege and Meinong came
in their own way to analogous views. Russell was for some time
in correspondence with Meinong over the problem of how logical
data could be said to be real. Of numbers, relations and Homeric
gods Russell maintained that they all have being, for if they were
not entities of a kind, we could make no propositions about them.
There is something of a reaction here to Stuart Mill's reduction
of knowledge to psychological terms, rather like Husserl's reaction
to psychologism. Frege protested in a similar way against the
attempt to reduce mathematical entities to an activity of the
intellect.

Logical empiricism, however, was later to modify this position.
Meanings were to be viewed no longer as entities, but as a product,
a precipitate of logical distinctions. This may be compared with
the conception of the Vienna school that a concept is not to be
viewed as having a reality of its own, but seen as a function.
G. Ryle sees here one of the most significant differences between

logical empiricism and phenomenology. In a paper of 1932, Ryle
points out that thinkers like Moore, Russell and Wittgenstein, in
distinction from Frege, Meinong and Husserl, do not view meanings as comprising a third realm beside those of physical and
psychological objects. They are viewed as a certain style of operation performed with words. In a game of chess one may think of
the "castle" either as a sample of ivory or as a piece in the game
with which certain moves can be made. But the "meaning" of
this piece of ivory within the rules of the game is not something
apart from the material, as an entity in its own right—thus Ryle
in a paper written later on the history of the theory of meaning
in recent philosophy.

This throws clearer light on the objection, voiced by Ryle on
behalf of a number of related thinkers, against Husserl's concept
of intentionality. Husserl viewed intentionality as the "directedness" of consciousness toward something outside, namely, meanings
conceived as entities. But to speak, for example, of "the object
of Mr. Jones' wish" is to use a systematically misleading expression,
unless it be understood that it is not a kind of imaginary object
that is in mind, but a characteristic of the situation in which
Jones finds himself, and of the changes in it which he desires. An
expression like "consciousness of . . ." is therefore better replaced
with "knowledge of . . . ," that is, knowing that something is
the case. To sum up these considerations of Ryle in relation to
what has previously been discussed: the intentional object must
be reduced to the meaning, and this in its turn is an expression
of the way in which something is known.

Similar ideas on intentionality, involving a rejection of Husserl's
views, were put forward sometime before by Schlick and Carnap.
Schlick would recognize intentionality only as a logical relation
between various data. Carnap went into far greater detail. The
concept of intentionality indicates the relation between an experience and the object with which it is concerned. This relation
implies a non-identity between experience and the object of experience, which does not mean, however, that intentionality is something entirely on its own. It is one of the many relations between
an element and a structure, which can be logically discerned. Ac-

cordingly, the relation of a particular color to the colored object is that of a color-element to the structure to which it logically belongs. Thus the "experience of a tree" falls logically under the structure "tree."

For a proper understanding of Carnap here we need to add two remarks. First, that his own discussions center upon the intentionality of sensory perception, while those of Ryle (considerably later) are concerned with the intentionality of logical essences. For Husserl, the one kind of intentionality flowed naturally out of the other: by way of "ideation" one can move from the (sensory) observation of a tree to the (non-sensory) intuition of the essential features of a tree. Second, Carnap does not mean to speak of intentionality as a relation between the tree-experience and the actual tree "over there," as the object of observation, which is more or less Brentano's idea. No, his remarks must be seen within the framework of his logical "syntax," in which he compares the structures of language; he does not, therefore, talk of the relation between the psychological world (tree-experience) and the physical world (tree), but of the logical relation between structures of language ("tree-experience" and "tree").

It becomes evident from all this that philosophy in the logical positivist sense is never a description of this or any higher reality. One could perhaps speak of "normative" philosophy, not because it uncovers "norms" or "values," but because it indicates certain rules for a logical and clear use of language. Wittgenstein was later to say much the same thing in his investigations into the foundations of mathematics where he speaks of mathematics as normative. Mathematics forms a network of norms, not as a kind of "ultra-physics" concerned with the discovery of ideal norms, but as an indication of the rules one must follow if one is to attain certain results. Various philosophers have expressed this by saying that the point of such rules is to decide what exactly is to be understood by "argument," "thought" and so on.

An illustration that is frequently used is that of a game of chess. Here too there is talk of a "must," not in the sense that one is physically compelled to make certain moves, but to point out the fact that if one does not intend to abide by the rules then whatever one does it will not be chess. Ryle has taken up this image more recently to make clear once again that the business of philosophy is not with the description of natural operations or facts. The logical analyses that belong to philosophy are quite independent of whatever may be discovered empirically. This applies, in fact, to everything we speak of as "thought." Ryle refers to the error of investigating thought as a natural process, rather like digestion, and of supposing to discover thereby the logical nature of thought. Certainly, one may investigate thought as a natural process. This has been done by the thought-psychology and depth-psychology of Freud, which have yielded valuable data about thought as a natural process. But thought as a logical process is something else. Not that this other aspect is isolated empirically or temporally from the natural process. Thought does not consist of pieces unnaturally stuck together. It is more like a game of golf or of chess. It is natural, but it is also more than this: the observance of certain rules. The philosophical analysis of the meanings of particular words and sentences is directed precisely to these rules. We may recall how Husserl and Schlick compared thought with a calculating-machine.

In his evaluation of phenomenology (in the above mentioned paper of 1932) Ryle maintains that in Husserl it amounts to a logical investigation on *a priori* grounds, not, therefore, on grounds of induction or of the data of empirical psychology. Husserl is well aware of the difference between the psychological and the philosophical investigation of consciousness; in the latter case "consciousness" has the meaning of a logical structure, not of a natural datum. Ryle remarks in passing that this does not proscribe the use of special empirical cases for the illustration of philosophical argumentation, provided one does not suppose that they furnish its logical foundation, its *ergo*. The remark is important, for the logical investigation of phenomenology, as of the more recent linguistic analysis, has been constantly reinvigorated, indeed empirically tested, by numerous concrete examples in the light of which the analyses have progressed.

A second point to the credit of phenomenology is, according to Ryle, the attempt to analyze, from a logical point of view, what is meant by a psychological proposition, and this irrespective of whether in the case in question the proposition is true or false. And rightly, for it is not for philosophy to give information about reality; its business is to analyze the general forms of propositions that do, purportedly, give such information. This analysis of the content of a proposition, irrespective of its truth or falsity, has from the start played a dominant role in logical empiricism. It finds its clearest formulation in Wittgenstein's TRACTATUS. He analyzes language in its composition of simple elements or signs. The signs are names the meaning of which are the objects—an idea that occurs also in Carnap when he deals with the relation of a proposition in which there is talk of a tree-experience, to the "tree." In a proposition the elementary meanings are brought together in such a way that it acquires a specific sense. And a proposition has sense only if it can be true or false. There are, of course, also propositions made up of other propositions in such a way that the truth-value is always positive, that is to say, that the composite proposition is a tautology. Wittgenstein speaks of tautology here—since it offers nothing new, no information, only clarification—as "lacking sense." This is not to say that a tautology is "nonsensical." But in general a proposition has sense (or is "meaningful," as others say) if it admits of being either true or false, that is, if it is verifiable. It is here a question of a factual proposition, or, as we might say, a contingent proposition. It is not, once again, a question of whether a proposition is true or false, for logical analysis is not concerned with the factual realization of a proposition, but with its structure, its sense, and thus with the proposition itself only to the extent that it *admits* of being either true or false. A proposition then says nothing of what a thing is, only of how it is, that is to say, in what relation it can function, as seen from a logical point of view. Wittgenstein speaks of the logical co-ordinates that are set out by this proposition and that determine a position in logical space. Whether or not such a position is actually occupied by a fact or thing *in concreto* only an empirical investigation (in science or ordinary observation) can decide; it lies beyond the bounds of the logical meaning-analysis of philosophy.

There is in all this a certain "aloofness" from what is factually and empirically given. The tension between logical analysis and factual description becomes apparent nevertheless, and with it emerges the classical philosophical problem of the relation between knowledge and reality. How does one arrive at the elementary components out of which a proposition is made? Some hold the view that these elements can be defined by reference to their objects. The name "King's College" acquires meaning by the speaker's pointing to it and saying: "That is King's College." Other philosophers of this school, such as Ayer, reject these "ostensive definitions" so-called, on the grounds that the elements involved are not logically determinable, but are tied up with the total empirical situation in which a speaker addresses himself to another person. Wittgenstein's view is that elementary components or names, cannot be defined. The proposition itself exhibits its meaning and does not acquire it through an "ostensive definition" or through affirmation of what the proposition contains. In his TRACTATUS Wittgenstein puts this within a metaphysical framework by speaking of the conformity of language with reality, which is evident in the whole structure of language. As will become clear in one of the later chapters, this problem of the point of contact between logical structures and factual reality becomes increasingly urgent and leads, in the case of Carnap for example, to a surrender of the narrower formalist standpoint.

However, there is one issue in this phase of logical positivism that needs to be gone into further, especially where it touches on the logical status of the laws of physics. The views expressed by various philosophers of this circle on the law of gravitation can well serve as an illustration here. A physical law of this kind has two distinguishable aspects. There is first the logical aspect; this concerns the formal conditions of such a law: such things as logical consistency, what Schlick calls the moment of "discretion." There are then the material conditions which form an altogether different aspect, for these are bound up with the empirical data which decide whether the truth-conditions of such a law are fulfilled to a greater or lesser degree. We are here concerned with Schlick's "continuity" and Wittgenstein's "contingency"—the contingency of a position marked by logical co-ordinates being actually occupied.

Schlick lays stress on his "continuity" by speaking of the element of probability that enters the picture when it comes to establishing empirically the extent to which the formal rules are materially verified. The new theory of gravitation must in this sense—according to Schlick in 1919, thus after the general relativity theory—be regarded as more probable than Newton's. However, this recognition of probability is itself categorical. Schlick draws a parallel here with causality. As to the causal relation as such there can be no doubt; the doubt is with regard to the question of whether causality can be applied in nature universally.

Wittgenstein compares the logical structure of Newtonian mechanics with a network—an image used also by other thinkers, such as Bergson and Eddington, for the elucidation of natural laws. Wittgenstein's use of the comparison is somewhat peculiar. The network serves to indicate the "logically discrete" in "continuity," to use the terminology of Schlick. The net is spread over a white surface bearing some irregularly formed black marks. The idea is then to establish for each pane in the network whether it is white or black. This might be easier as the meshes of the net are finer, so that a pane would almost invariably be either wholly white or wholly black. It could be, however, that a somewhat coarser net with triangular meshes would give a better effect than a finer net with rectangular meshes. Whatever can be said about the net— the relations that occur in the network, and so on—has no bearing as yet on reality, being confined to the formal system. It begins to touch on reality, says Wittgenstein, as soon as one observes that one net works better than another. That one is able to describe the physical world in terms of Newtonian mechanics for example, tells us nothing *about that world;* it tells us only that it admits of mechanical description, or that such a description can be better performed in terms of one mechanics than it can be in terms of another.

Thus, the philosophers of logical positivism have framed in their various ways a formal, logical language to furnish a clarification of phenomena. In this they have tried to be detached from the empirical, as far as this is possible, without its ever being entirely eliminated.

Brief Bibliography

G. Anscombe, *An Introduction to Wittgenstein's Tractatus,* London, 1959.

A. J. Ayer, *Language, Truth, Logic,* rev. ed., London, 1946 (1st ed., 1936).

M. Black, *A Companion to Wittgenstein's Tractatus,* Cambridge, 1964.

R. Carnap, *Der logische Aufbau der Welt,* Berlin, 1928.

———, *Scheinprobleme der Philosophie,* Berlin, 1928. Both volumes in one, Hamburg, 1961.

———, *The Logical Syntax of Language,* London, 1937. 2nd ed., 1949.

G. Frege, "Ueber Sinn und Bedeutung," *Zeitschrift f. Philos. und philos. Kritik,* vol. 100(1892).

J. Griffin, *Wittgenstein's Logical Atomism,* Oxford, 1964.

V. Kraft, *The Vienna Circle,* New York, 1954.

A. Maslow, *A Study in Wittgenstein's Tractatus,* Berkeley, Calif., 1961.

R. von Mises, *Positivism,* Cambridge, Mass., 1951.

B. Russell, "On Denoting," *Mind,* vol. 14(1905).

———, *The Philosophy of Logical Atomism,* (1918-19), Minneapolis, Minn., 1949.

———, *Inquiry into Meaning and Truth,* London, 1940.

G. Ryle, "Systematically Misleading Expressions," *Proceedings of the Aristotelian Society,* New Series, vol. 32(1932).

———, "Phenomenology," Supplement 11 of the same.

M. Schlick, *Raum und Zeit in der gegenwärtigen Physik,* Berlin, 1917.

———, *Allgemeine Erkenntnislehre,* Berlin, 1918.

———, *Gesammelte Aufsätze 1926-1936,* ed. by F. Waismann, Vienna, 1938.

———, *Fragen der Ethik,* Vienna, 1940.

E. Stenius, *Wittgenstein's Tractatus,* Oxford, 1960.

L. Wittgenstein, *Notebooks 1914-1916,* ed. by G. von Wright and G. Anscombe, Oxford, 1961.

Tractatus Logico-philosophicus, English tr. by C. Ogden, introduction by B. Russell, London, 1922. New ed. with English tr. by D. Pears and B. McGuinness, London, 1963.

Chapter Five

Analytical Reduction and Factual Existence

IN THE foregoing chapter we referred briefly to Wittgenstein's conception of tautologies as logical laws. A tautology was not for him what it was for Kant—an analytical judgment, a judgment in which the predicate is already contained in the subject, as in "a circle is round," for example—but a set of propositions, equally balanced, as it were, at every level. That is to say that, regardless of the truth or falsity of each of the elementary propositions, the composite proposition is always true. A simple example: "it is raining or it is not raining," "p V -p." From this we learn nothing in fact about the weather, according to Wittgenstein. A tautology fully occupies logical space; a proposition that can be either true or false, that is contingent therefore and not necessary, marks one specific point in logical space. Here is a statement about the factual state of affairs (or "atomic fact," as in the earlier translation of Wittgenstein's TRACTATUS) that may decide whether the constellation affirmed in the proposition exists, and thus whether the proposition is true.

It is against this background that we must look at subsequent attempts at the formalization of language. Formalization here means a setting aside of the content of language and limiting oneself entirely to logical or structural rules. This is not to say that one is limited to a tautological system, but rather that one analyzes contingent propositions still further so as to bring recalcitrant facts so far as possible within the orbit of logical syntax. Moreover, the question of reality is discarded, so that a certain resemblance with what Husserl called the phenomenological reduction is here unmistakable. This is true of Carnap in particular, who had worked for a while with Husserl and was well informed of Husserl's logical investigations.

Husserl had thought for some time of the possibility of a purely logical grammar. Carnap undoubtedly benefited from this, as is evident from his study of 1934 on logical syntax. A philosopher much influenced by Carnap, Y. Bar-Hillel, has pointed out innumerable cases in which Carnap was able to improve on the ideas of Husserl. He too criticized Husserl's idea of evidence, as being, in this case, a kind of linguistic intuition. For this reason Husserl's investigation was too closely bound up with the language at his disposal, German. What was indeed important in Husserl was his distinction between nonsense (*Unsinn*), as in a mere accumulation of words, and counter-sense (*Widersinn*) or absurdity, as in "the circle is square." This distinction corresponds with that made by Carnap between "rules of formation" and "rules of transformation."

Such distinctions within a logical grammar give rise to the problem—in Husserl's words—of what is physically possible. Carnap distinguishes, in a study on physical language (of 1931), between "system language" and "protocol language," the second being derivable from the first. If this derivation were impossible, then system language would be meaningless. The question of pure logical grammar, of the agreement of thought with itself, proves to be bound up with the question of verifiability, of the agreement of thought with things. This manner of expression would be misleading, however, if logical investigation were supposed to resolve itself into the classical question as to where language and reality, thought and being, meet. No; the many discussions that have centered on the verification principle lose their real significance if not viewed as part of the larger problem of the meaningfulness of "system language."

Now this comes clearly into prominence in the work of Carnap. It was in about 1930 that Carnap and Neurath advanced the thesis of "protocol language" as a necessary component of any language that could claim to speak of reality. Protocol language, which would include a statement like "the temperature of liquid n rises between the times t' and t'' by p degrees," is not, as some have supposed, an attempt to base knowledge on sensory experience. Carnap's intention is precisely to clear every such basis out of the way so as to gain a clear view of structures open to logical analysis. Protocol statements are therefore based on "experiences" (*Erlebnisse*).

What is here meant by "experiences"? With reference to what Husserl called the "mathematics of experiences" and to Meinong's "theory of objects" (the so-called *Gegenstandstheorie*), Carnap developed the concept of "experience" as the primary datum in the logical structure of knowledge. The idea is put forward in his book THE LOGICAL CONSTRUCTION OF THE WORLD (1928). What is the "given" on which scientific and logical conceptualization is founded? This question Carnap regards as central to both his and Husserl's investigations. He applies the phenomenological reduction in order to bring this "given" into view. His use of terms like "bracketing" (*Einklammerung*) and "*epochē*" (*i.e.*, suspension of judgment) are derived directly from Husserl. For Carnap is also concerned to get behind the distinction between the "real" and the "unreal." It is there that phenomena are to be found in their most elementary structure. What then are these phenomena? They are phenomena as experiences (*Erlebnisse*). That experiences are here to be understood not in the psychological sense but as logical structure, becomes increasingly clear from his analyses.

Experiences are to be analyzed *prior* to the claim being made— or denied—that they refer to reality. That is to say, there is as yet no distinction of meaning here as would distinguish, for example, hallucination from observation. Carnap uses the word "constitution" in order to point out that the affirmation of real/unreal is a distinction that is logically posterior. Only experiences as such are given. Carnap speaks of the "stream of experience" (*Erlebnisstrom*) which has as yet no subject. Here is a methodical (!) solipsism, because, from a logical point of view, an experience is related to an "I" only when there is talk of the experiences of others. But both "I" and the "other" are "constituted" (at a logically higher level) only from the stream of pure given experiences. It is, says Carnap, citing Nietzsche, a formulation of our grammatical habit, by which for every act we posit an agent. Thus Carnap, like Mach before him, posits an "I-less" point of departure for the logical construction of knowledge; and in this he deviates from people like Husserl and

Russell. Accordingly, the correlation between subject and object, suggested by the structure of language and especially in the subject-predicate form, proves to be absent from what, logically speaking, is originally given.

In fact, of course, Carnap may know of these experiences only as *his* experiences. He speaks of the constitution (that is, the logical construction) of real and unreal, of "I" and the "other," as from *"my"* experiences. One could ask here how there can be talk about "my" in a context where the distinction between "I" and the "other" has not yet presented itself. The answer would be that one has to distinguish between the two possible points of departure for analysis: that which can be logically identified and that which can be psychologically or factually identified. It is the distinction already pointed out by Kant, in terms of what is given *de jure* on the one hand, and what is given *de facto* on the other. Thus Carnap analyzes *de facto* his own, factually given experiences in order to uncover *de jure* the structure of a subjectless stream of experience.

Yet the difficulty in all this of freeing the logical and necessary from the empirical and contingent betrays itself still. This becomes apparent when Carnap asks if this concentration on directly given experiences does not lead to subjectivism. Are one's experiences essentially no different from those of another—even when viewed in their elementary logical structure, thus still without a subject? The answer Carnap gives is still another attempt to separate the logical from the empirical. In this logical investigation, he argues, we must look not for the material of the stream of experience but for its structure. This answer is important in two respects. First, because here, as elsewhere in his works, he lays stress on the fact that philosophical language deals with structures: logical syntax has for its object not empirical data, such as belong to the sciences, but the rules of language, by which such data are ordered. Second, it is evident from this answer that the word "experiences" (or rather "my experiences") has to be understood in a very specific sense. These are certainly no factual experiences admitting of psychological investigation. Here again they ask for an analysis of structures. This helps to make clear that what was meant by the above-mentioned protocol rules was not rules for sensory experiences, but rules in the formal, non-material sense just indicated, as with Carnap's "experiences."

That Carnap's ideas, precisely on the logical construction of the world, are very much in line with Husserl's project in the phenomenological reduction, should now be plain. But the difference too is apparent, a difference characteristic of the contrast between phenomenology and logical positivism: Carnap speaks about a stream of experience without content, as formal structures; Husserl tries to bring the content of experience within his methodological field of vision. Hence his inclination to speak about "intuiting," "essences" and "evidence." Related to this is the difference between the "pure grammar" of Husserl and the "logical syntax" of Carnap. A detailed study of Carnap's analyses reveals, for the rest, how closely in line they are with what Husserl had drawn up in his IDEAS, Vol. II (not published until 1952). Carnap describes, for example, the logical structure of the visual world. This has as yet only two dimensions. There can be talk of a third dimension only when tactile experiences and kinaesthetic experiences in general have part in the spacial constitution. Only at this level is it possible to constitute what is known as the "outside world" and "reality." Only then is there talk of "space" in the physical sense. This is other than geometric "space," which is part of logic and system language, a scheme for ordering data, but not the structure of what is given empirically. One could say, as we have earlier shown, that geometric "space" may become space in the narrower sense by way of application to physical space. This means that the formal structures of the stream of experience, which come to light in this logical analysis, form no part of a self-contained logic, but properly concern the construction of the empirical world—viewed as methodological bracketing. In other words, the investigation concerns synthetic statements, including those about reality, rather than analytical, merely formal statements. The logical structure of this is studied in great detail by Carnap; this paragraph is but a brief illustration of his study.

We have devoted some attention to Carnap, not only because at one stage he shows a clear parallel in method with Husserl, but also because he brings into the open the ambition of all logical positivists, namely, to go beyond the bounds of logic and to explore the empirical world as a whole by way of a structural analysis. This entails a certain tension, as appears from the use of the word "experiences." These form the elementary level of all that is given empirically, yet they are viewed at the same time in terms of structure, or, as Carnap frequently puts it, quite apart from the historical "I" and historical reality. One can draw a parallel here with what Carnap elsewhere says about his distinction between object sentences and syntactic sentences: just as " '5' is not a thing, but a number" proves to be a pseudo-object sentence, which has to be replaced by the syntactic sentence " '5' is not a thing-word, but a number-word," so have Carnap's statements about experiences to be conceived, not as object sentences—which would simply require psychological investigation—but as syntactic sentences.

Connected with this is the much discussed "physicalism," the conception, developed by Carnap and Neurath among others, that all protocol statements can be translated into the language of physics. It concerns the requirement for a linguistic transformation. It would be a serious misunderstanding to suppose that, because statements about physical experiences were to be reduced to physical observations, this was a type of materialism. The ideas of "physicalism," developed a few years after the study on the logical construction of the world, should be seen as a demand of a purely linguistic, and in no sense a metaphysical (materialistic) nature. It is not a matter, even then, of a statement about the factual content of, say, physical phenomena, but a matter of a "rule of transformation" that would lead to results as pure and intersubjective as possible. This attempt has been burdened with the same kind of difficulties as arose with the idea of protocol statements: with a statement like "at this very moment I observe a red color," do I not fall back on the subjective experience-of-red? Schlick had argued that here, at the final limit, there was given an inexpressible experience, that was then embodied in a protocol statement, and thus in every verification. Is then this ultimate limit of inexpressible experience the point of contact between language and reality, between thought and being? Wittgenstein too had made reference to inexpressibility, where it concerned the conformity of language with reality—a conformity, though, that could show itself. Physicalism seeks another solution by way of a prescription for transformation, such as could guarantee the intersubjectivity of verifying statements. Once again, however, this rule should be viewed syntactically; it offers no statement on the conformity, or otherwise, of language with reality, as if the status of perceptions and experiences was an object.

We have already shown that the tension involved in Carnap's (and others') setting aside empirical experience lies precisely in the structure of this experience (as "my experiences" in the elementary structural sense). In point of fact, this amounts to an extreme formalist standpoint, in which the content of experience and empirical verification are reduced to structures, logical constructions and rules of transformation. One of the most penetrating critics of this view has been A. J. Ayer. His criticism was influenced by Russell's ideas, which were far more metaphysical, for Russell had wanted to keep well in view the question of the conformity of language with reality. At one stage of his development he answered this question, as did his one-time pupil Wittgenstein, in terms of the doctrine that the elementary structures of logic correspond to the elementary states of affairs, the so-called "atomic facts" of reality.

Ayer takes a different line here, but he does align himself with the attempt to discover the connection of language with reality, a connection implied, for instance, in the verification principle. At an early stage, therefore, he leveled criticism against the views of Carnap, his physicalism especially, even though he still inclined to the closely associated views of behaviorism, with their concern for the description of internal experience. His views on Carnap could hardly be better expressed than in the formulation which Ayer was to give them much later.

The background to Carnap's method, according to Ayer, is his now famous distinction between 1. object sentences, 2. pseudo-object sentences, and 3. syntactic sentences. Ayer adds a fourth class: quasi-syntactic sentences. These are statements which *qua* form are entirely syntactic, but which, logically viewed, are semantic, that is to say, which refer beyond syntax to something else; just the reverse of what proved to be the case with pseudo-object sentences. Now, this happens to be the case with all Carnap's statements about experiences. These are so construed by Carnap that they appear to be purely syntactic, and thus purely formal. But viewed logically, their meaning is not defined by their form (syntactically), but by their reference to empirical experience. This means that the tension to which we have referred is considered by Ayer to be, strictly speaking, logically intolerable: the logical structure of the world and the physicalist "requirement" (intended, though it was, as a mere rule of transformation) imply, nonetheless, a relation to the factual, empirical world. Indeed, the further development of Carnap's own thought points in the same direction. For the verification principle gave rise to a whole crop of questions about what precisely was meant by the "method of verification," a method which had to decide, after all, the meaning of statements issuing from it. Carnap introduced the tolerance principle, by which everyone was free, within a certain frame of reference, to decide for himself what kind of verifiability was appropriate to his system. A still more elastic conception was defended by H. Reichenbach, who distinguished various kinds of verifiability, such as physical, logical, and even trans-empirical.

More important still is a second point. In about 1935 the logician A. Tarski applied himself directly to the problem of the point of contact between language and reality by reformulating, in brief and in technical, logical terms, the correspondence theory of truth— truth as the conformity of thought with actual constellations. This reformulation is semantic; it offers, that is, an interpreted system of language; an uninterpreted calculus, on the other hand, would be a purely syntactic system of language. Here Carnap found a point of departure and developed a semantics. In so doing he abandoned his formalist standpoint. While it is true that formalism of all kinds can find its way into a semantic system, and that good use can be made there of logical signs, the theme of semantics is precisely the relation of words to things.

We cannot elaborate here on the interesting changes that have taken place in the development of logical positivism. But we can summarize them, perhaps, by speaking of a sharper awareness of the relativity of a closed logical system. What had been understood by "directly given experience," or by "verification," or even by an "analytical proposition" and a "tautology," proved to be partly determined by the historical and cultural horizon of perception and thought. Perception is no mechanical, photographic activity, and logical thought is evidently not a timeless network, spread over the world of fact and change. Carnap speaks, for instance, of the cultural circle within which alone one can speak of the consistency, the logical identity, of a system of statements. Other problems too are now to be seen in a different light. There is the view of Carnap and Schlick on intentionality as a syntactic datum, that is to say, as the relation of a certain element of language (*e.g.*, "tree-experience") to another structural datum (*e.g.*, "tree"). This now proves to be inadequate, because this intentionality cannot be limited to the syntactic, but has semantic implications. Here again, as in other respects with Husserl's phenomenological reduction, a point of friction is felt between the uniform demands of logical rules on the one hand, and empirically changing things and facts on the other. This means, at the same time, that logical analysis has moved into a new phase, just as it will finally move toward the analytical description of everyday language and of the human world of history.

Brief Bibliography

A. J. Ayer, ed., *Logical Positivism*, Glencoe, Ill., 1959. Contains the English translations of some of the articles mentioned below.

F. Barone, *Il neopositivismo logico*, Turin, 1953.

R. Carnap, "Die physikalische Sprache als Universalsprache der Wissenschaft," *Erkenntnis*, vol. 2(1931-32).

———, "Psychologie in physikalischer Sprache," *ibid.*, vol. 3(1932-33).

————, "Ueber Protokollsätze," *ibid.*, vol. 2(1931-32) and vol. 3(1932-33).

————, *Testability and Meaning*, 1936-37; reprinted, New Haven, Conn., 1950.

I. Copi and R. Beard, ed., *Essays on Wittgenstein's Tractatus*, London, 1966.

J. Feibleman, *Inside the Great Mirror. A Critical Examination of the Philosophy of Russell, Wittgenstein, and Their Followers.* London, 1958.

A. Müller, *Ontologie in Wittgensteins Tractatus*, Bonn, 1967.

O Neurath, "Protokollsätze," *Erkenntnis*, vol. 3(1932-33).

————, "Radikaler Physikalismus und 'wirkliche Welt,'" *ibid.*, vol. 4(1933-34).

M. Schlick, "Meaning and Verification," *Philosophical Review*, vol. 44(1936).

W. Stegmüller, *Hauptströmungen der Gegenwartsphilosophie*, 3rd ed., Stuttgart, 1965.

A. Tarski, "The Semantic Conception of Truth," *Philosophy and Phenomenological Research*, vol. 4(1944). Also contained in H. Feigl and W. Sellars, ed., *Readings in Philosophical Analysis*, New York, 1953.

J. Weinberg, *An Examination of Logical Positivism*, London, 1936.

Chapter Six

A First Confrontation: Operational or Intuitive Meaning?

Phenomenology and logical positivism can, from a certain point of view, be seen as antipodal: a more lofty, synthetic and speculative method stands diametrically opposed to a more sober, analytical and empirical one. Yet, on closer inspection, they prove to bear striking resemblance. One will notice in particular how these two currents of thought have proceeded from a similar starting-point. This will be more fully explained in the present chapter. Later, in a second and final confrontation, it will become evident that agreement and disagreement are to be found also in the most recent developments of these philosophical schools, though their center of gravity will be seen in each case to have shifted.

The first period in the development of both these currents can be characterized, by contrast with later developments, by its preoccupation with method, and in the method with a philosophical program. The intention in each case was to present a renewal of the whole of philosophical and scientific thought. Sometimes even this took on the form of a manifesto. Logical positivism arose from the proclamation of the unity of the sciences and Husserl wrote across his banner "Phenomenology as a Rigorous Science." Both were imbued with the sense of having a revolutionary task to perform. Philosophy had drifted into meaningless speculations, and logic in particular threatened to run around in the waters of empirical investigation, having sheered from the rigor and exactness of logical scientific reasoning.

Characteristic of the logical investigation of both schools is the standard of identity. The logical is a structure to which one may return again and again and which presents itself always as the same. The logical is definitive; it maps out clear definitions. Both Husserl and Schlick, for example, speak about the one logical meaning of a statement in, say, mathematics which may occur in a number of different forms: in observation or memory, in English or German, etc. This logical identity at the same time implies consistency, for a system of propositions is found then to be governed by rules which make possible the reducing of the one proposition to the other. This logical consistency (*Einstimmigkeit*), however, also involves sharp distinctions. Each concept is, logically, not linguistically, speaking, wholly distinct from another. That is to say that, from a logical point of view, concepts are insoluble; they may well enclose or partly comprise each other in certain respects, but this is then determined by unambiguous, logical rules.

All this applies not only to pure, non-empirical relations, but also to the description of empirical reality. Verification in the logical positivist method is precisely the identity of the one content of many statements made by a number of subjects, as observers of physical event, for example. Schlick speaks of the many, sometimes qualitatively various, statements (*e.g.*, about an observed object, about the physical health of the person who made the first statement, about the logical stringency of the scientific language used by the second speaker, etc.), which all affirm the same propositional content (e.g., "the house in the park is red"). Husserl refers to the possibility of misrepresenting a proposition or of mistaking what is said in a proposition in regard to the facts at one's disposal—circumstances he sharply distinguishes from the logical status of that proposition.

Of interest in this connection is the idea of "probability." Husserl refers to the probability that comes into play when one considers the extent to which logical laws are empirically applicable. Meinong, who, though not belonging to the phenomenological school, was working independently with similar ideas, had tried at the beginning of the century to revise the concept of probability in logical terms by indicating its various relations. Wittgenstein did the same in his TRACTATUS when he considered the determination of the degree of probability arising from the mutual relations between non-tautological propositions. In short, it is probability as a yard-stick for logical applicability that is here at issue; logical analysis is threading its way into the contingency of given phenomena.

These logical investigations stand out in sharp relief against the many attempts to base scientific method on what is given empirically. The psychological reduction of knowledge especially evokes the protests of both Husserl and the members or associates of the Vienna Circle. Accordingly, anti-psychologism is a feature these schools hold in common. Thus Ryle can say that the method of logical positivism, like that of phenomenology, is "*a priori*," that is to say, is based neither on factual induction nor on the data of empirical psychology. Both investigate "consciousness," not as natural consciousness, but as "meaning," as logical structure. Logical investigation differs from all factual or natural research precisely by the identities which it discovers in the changing, factual data. Husserl demonstrated how one can unveil the logical structures within a multiplicity of natural and variable data, and how these structures overlap one another and thus display identity and consistency (*Einstimmigkeit*). Schlick speaks of the "discretion" of logic, that, of the sharp defining of, for example, "true" and "false," or, in Wittgenstein's picture, of black and white panes. The discriminating capacity is different in kind from the merging lines and continuous transitions which occur at the natural (physical and psychological) level. The picture of the calculating machine with its physical and its arithmetical laws is used by Husserl as well as by Schlick. Similarly, both schools make analogous distinctions between natural or physical space and geometric "space," which refers to a wide field of possible logical operations.

There is a large measure of agreement, therefore, in what we may call the methodological point of departure. But here too—and this is a second point of confrontation—there is an obvious difference in approach. The difference becomes evident as soon as we raise the question of how it is possible to reach beyond empirical, changing and natural data so as to grasp the structural meaning, the logical identification, the discrete concept. Both schools would answer by referring to a process, but the way they described it would be different in each case.

Logical positivist thinkers generally would describe the logical process as indicating relations and combining distinguishable elements (Carnap, Schlick). This would mean at the same time the drawing up and analyzing of the rules which govern such a process (Wittgenstein). In this description of the logical process the view is focused on what occurs at the level of logical language. The concept can thus be sharply distinguished from the (psychological) representation. The process does not take place in the subject, but at the level of the objective structures of language—language, not in the empirical and changeable sense, but in the logical sense of syntax and grammar.

Phenomenological thinkers would describe the logical process as a special activity of the subject. A grouping of verbal signs is to be conceived as a "meaning," an arrangement of lines on paper as proof of a geometrical theorem. In this connection Husserl speaks of "apperception," the logical process by which a subject can assimilate natural data as logical meanings. He also distinguishes the concept from the psychological representations which, from a logical point of view, *attend* it, but which never make up its content. For Husserl this implies more than the separation and combination of the logical elements of language. Not only at the objective pole (in language, in data), but at the subjective pole also (in man as the subject of knowledge) something takes place which is not to be identified with natural (physical or psychological) processes. Indeed, the logical distinctions at the objective pole are made possible only by a special concentration and intention on the part of the subject.

Evidently, it is more than a question of emphasis here. In the first edition of his LOGICAL INVESTIGATIONS (1900) Husserl offers no theory of the subject in the sense of an "I," though such a theory is later to play a significant part in his work. What has been of significance from the very beginning is the activity of the subject in the sense we have just explained. Here Husserl differs from the logical positivists, but also from a thinker like Meinong who would in other respects be closer to him. He does not portray the logical process as a result of what, empirically speaking, goes on in the mind. As the foregoing chapters have shown, the logical subject must be conceived purely as a cognitive function in the structural, non-psychological sense. In the phenomenological reduction especially it is evident that this subject is to be sharply distinguished from the entire natural world, the world of natural objects and human subjects. How the logical structural subject is to be related to the empirical man, to the natural "I," is a problem that Husserl is never quite able to surmount. To sum up, we may say that the logical process, emphasized strongly on both sides, is described by neo-positivist thinkers largely in terms of objectivity, and by Husserl more in terms of structural subjectivity.

A third point of confrontation, the concept of "evidence," draws the dividing line further, showing up the contrasts more clearly. But here too there are certain likenesses, though these tend to remain in the background. Husserl portrays evidence as occurring with the direct apprehension of logical patterns. This is in line with his portrayal of subjectivity as active in every logical process. It is as much in line with the charge brought against him by neo-positivist thinkers that he is guilty at this point of subjectivism and even of psychologism. Evidence is a feeling in which it is possible to be mistaken and which is quite independent of the logical status of a statement.

Yet the case is not so simple. The charge from the neo-positivist side hardly does justice to Husserl's carefully qualified views on evidence, which, he insists, is not to be equated with the feeling of evidence. Husserl himself calls feelings of evidence subjective, attendant, and irrelevant to the analysis of what he means by evidence in the logical sense. In acts of perception, understanding and the like a subject directs its attention to an "object" (a thing, a mathematical proposition, a remembered event, etc.). This is not to say that the object in question is immediately given in such an act. Husserl gives a detailed description of the "fulfillment" (*Erfül-lung*) that here takes place and that can be understood as the degree in which, logically speaking, the object is present in the act. One could say that his sixth logical investigation, where Husserl enlarges on this idea of "fulfillment," forms his descriptive phenomenological psychology, provided one does not take "psychology" to mean an investigation of empirical, psychologically describable data, but rather, in the Husserlian sense, a logical analysis of cognitive processes, even though these are not here treated according to the method he was later to develop as the phenomenological reduction. The importance of the analysis of the "fulfillment" of logical acts has been brought to the attention of the English-speaking world in the work of J. N. Findlay.

Fulfillment in the logical sense plays a large part in the process by which a logical structure is identified in a number of empirical forms. It is closely connected, therefore, with evidence, as explained in previous chapters. Husserl speaks of a "fulfillment synthesis" (*Erfüllungssynthesis*) where separate data (*e.g.*, perceptions, memories, acts of mathematical conception) coincide in the one logical structure (*e.g.*, a mathematical theorem) which logically "fills" them. Evidence then appears to complete the process. Now the structure or meaning intended is given as such, and acts originally empty are filled through logical identification.

Clearly, this is more than a question of psychological and subjective experiences. Husserl tries to separate completely the two senses of evidence. One may recall the distinction he made between the real object, with such attendant functions as the feeling of evidence and the fact that a proposition is either true or false, and, on the other hand, the object of the logical act. And this logical object, it appears, is unaffected by psychological feelings and factual verification, though it must indeed *admit* of being either true or false. Mistakes affect the real object, and leave the logical content untouched.

Husserl's analyses, even where they deal with the nature of "evidence," turn out, on closer inspection, to be rather more logical and less psychological than one at first would suspect. The critique of neo-positivist thinkers at this point somewhat misfired. Yet the treatment of the concept of evidence brings to light a real and characteristic difference of opinion. What is more striking is that the difference becomes apparent in the very thesis which these schools hold in common, namely, that the logical status of propositions is quite independent of questions of fact and thus of the question of whether a particular proposition is true or false. The logical method investigates meanings in a sphere detached from empirical experience. Wittgenstein speaks of logical space and of propositions as the logical coordinates by which a point may be marked within space where something can be affirmed (or denied) to be the case. Phenomenology as well as logical positivism removes every logical network from the vicissitudes (contingency) of the natural world.

Now, it is precisely in this common thesis that the difference between them appears. If a composite proposition presents the truth-value in all cases as "true," one may call this tautology a logical law—as we have said in connection with Wittgenstein. In Husserl's case too one may speak of tautologies. Evidence itself, as a fulfillment of a logical expectation and as a mere identification of the same structure, implies a kind of tautology. This too we discussed in the previous chapter. The two schools use often the same illustrations, such as, for example, the axioms of mathematics and statements to the effect that something may at the same time be red and round, but not red and green.

The great difference lies in this: Husserl speaks of evidence and also of a direct insight into the truth of such a statement; Wittgenstein, speaking here for most logical positivists, says that logic can look after itself and dispense with every form of intuition or evidence. The opposition to Husserl's concept of evidence is thus understandable: "evidence" is entirely superfluous; it only hampers the use of a logical method. Why does Husserl think evidence so important at the point where the logical positivists consider it to be a disruption of logical clarity? The answer can be given in simple form by saying that the logical laws or tautologies in the positivist doctrine are trivial. This is not to say that tautological systems are of no significance or that they provide no stimulus for scientific thought. No, statements of this kind are trivial in the sense that they say nothing out of the ordinary—no metaphysical truth, no special intuition or evidence. Logical work consists in saying no more and no less than the obvious. One analyzes and discloses what is already implied in the field of logical operations.

With Husserl the case is rather different. The tautologies are for him the formulation of a logical law, which is directly given as such in that formulation. In this respect the division between the logical status of tautologies, of logical laws in the narrower sense, and that of the logical status of a meaning, which, as a logical structure, can be discerned in contingent proposition or even in a perception (*e.g.*, "the house is large," irrespective of whether in fact the statement is true or false), is for Husserl less sharp. Even though he recognizes the distinction between analytic and synthetic propositions, he maintains in both cases that a logical structure can be directly grasped and is then *itself* (*es selbst*) present. In other words, the logically self-evident is not, in a sense, altogether "self-evidence" for, properly speaking, it requires an effort—psychological *and* logical —which Husserl often refers to as an "identifying synthesis." Logical method, therefore, is not to allow logic to look after itself, but to establish the identity of logical structures concealed under separate, empirical data. To sum up, one can say that for Husserl tautologies are more synthetic, for the logical positivists more analytic. But one must not conclude that what the one takes to be an analytic proposition the other takes to be a synthetic proposition; rather, the one emphasizes that a logical structure can sometimes be disclosed merely by the analysis of what is already given objectively in the elements and rules of language, while the other, in the very same case, emphasizes the identifying and synthesizing activity of the subject in such a disclosure of structures.

Husserl's ideas, one could say, to a certain extent anticipate on developments within analytical philosophy with respect to the distinction between analytic and synthetic judgments which could not be rigorously maintained. This matter will be discussed more extensively in the last chapter; for the present we merely wish to make the following remarks.

a. Several authors consider analytic judgments less "obvious" than adherents of logical positivism were wont to think. An analytic judgment gives no information because the predicate is contained in the subject of the judgment; in Kantian terms, it is a tautology, as, *e.g.*, "a circle is round." This, however, depends on the logical system one has accepted. "Water is H_2O" became an analytic judgment when science had gone through a long period of development. Likewise, tautologies in Wittgenstein's sense—as judgments that are always true on the basis of the truth-functions of the judgments of which they are composed—as "p or not-p," are based on the assumption of certain logical rules, such as the law of the excluded middle, as Wittgenstein himself points out. The analytical character of judgments, then, is connected with a wider context demanding a more synthetic view of logically consistent rules.

b. At the same time, it also becomes clearer that synthetic judgments are less based on purely contingent facts; in a scientific realm the interconnection between theoretical statements and the observation of facts is more than sheer contingency. Every observation and verification is guided by a theoretical project; in this sense such synthetic judgments have a more logically regulated, a more analytical character than was commonly assumed.

Both these points are more or less implied in the above-discussed views of Husserl. First of all, he draws attention to the synthetic activity of the subject, even in purely analytical judgments. Secondly, he points to the logical, "eternal" character of the structures which are contained in contingent judgments, i.e., synthetic judgments of observation, such as "that house is red." On the other hand, he incorporates all this in a realistic conception of general meanings (universals): these meanings (the "red house," the content of the theorem of Pythagoras, etc.) are given as such and exist, as it were, in themselves. It was only in a much later stage of his development that Husserl attempted to connect such meanings with the factually given life-world (Cf. Chapter Eight).

All this helps to explain why the logical positivist speaks about constructing relations and defining concepts by means of the intellect, or rather by means of the logical rules of operation, while Husserl speaks about intuiting and takes account of logical insight. The difference, connected with the point just mentioned, can be formulated as follows: for the logical positivist an analytical proposition and a tautology give no information. The analysis offers nothing new and its result is therefore self-evident. Husserl also recognizes the self-evident, as, for example, in mathematical theses, but the logically self-evident is so distinct from what, in the first instance, is given empirically, as to signify something new. The logical is itself present, Husserl repeatedly states, it is itself grasped. One could say that what is directly grasped as logically self-evident is, in a sense, "revealed." Hence the more synthetic nature of Husserl's logical laws in contrast to the purely analytical conception of the logical positivists. Hence too Husserl's talk of insight and logical intuition with respect both to logical laws and to the general structure, the *eidos,* that can be abstracted from the concretely perceived by means of the eidetic reduction. Hence, finally, that evidence for him is not in the least superfluous in the logical process.

The ascertainment of a logical structure is, for the logical positivists, the result of a purely analytical activity. For Husserl, and for thinkers akin to him, like Scheler and Meinong, one could say that this activity is "ostensive." This term is not used by the phenomenologists themselves, but it does occur among the neo-positivists. The term "ostensive definitions" is defended by some as referring to the manner in which one indicates the meaning of a name. To indicate the meaning of "apple" one points to an apple. This pointing is then conceived as "defining," because in this way a sign-structure acquires meaning. It is plain that such ostensive definitions play a part in forming experimental or synthetic propositions. Now, one could say that Husserl considered a kind of "ostensive definition" necessary for the discernment of logical structures, since logical identity and consistency are not simply given, but have to be detected by a difficult process of identification. Where the logical positivists emphasize the self-evidence of logical structures over against the variability and non-discretion of empirical reality (where also, according to many, only unpredictable ostensive definitions can be said to belong), Husserl emphasizes the effort that is required to specify logical certainties in contradistinction from natural, variable reality.

It has been necessary to deal with this point of difference in detail, not only because the distinction here is real, but also because the presentation of Husserl's standpoint by logical positivists is on the whole deficient and to accuse him of psychologism and mysticism is to misjudge his real intentions. Husserl's approach points to the fact that even an analysis of tautological systems can hardly be carried out automatically—a point which Wittgenstein will refer to much later in connection with mathematics.

After this somewhat lengthy confrontation we can discuss more briefly a number of other related differences. One of these is the idea of "meaning." We have already dealt with this to some extent in the previous chapters and we shall find it playing a part in further developments of both schools. There is, in the first place, a great measure of agreement on this point, as both schools of thought concern themselves, as Ryle has put it, with investigating the meaning of statements apart from their psychological or emotional value and apart from the factual question of whether a particular proposition is true or false. The question of meaning arises if a statement *admits* of being true or false, that is to say, if it makes sense. Here a sharp distinction is made in both schools between propositions that are purely logical (analytic, *vérités de raison*) and those that derive from experience (synthetic, *vérités de fait*). Husserl also makes a distinction between these propositions and sentences in which, for example, a command is contained and where, consequently, the question of truth or falsity cannot be put. In both schools the attempt is made to arrive at a methodological investigation that is not directed to empirical objects (these being left to the sciences), but to the propositions employed by scientific and other uses of language. The aim in view is a pure grammar (Husserl), a logical syntax (Carnap).

Here too we find the differences between the two views, which we can perhaps express in brief by stating that for Husserl "meaning" is a matter of content, and for the logical positivists more a matter of form. We have already mentioned the accusation of Bar-Hillel, who, in line with Carnap, considers Husserl's conception of a logical grammar to be too much bound to grammatical intuition and thus too much bound to his own native language. Husserl's logical grammar is, it is true, *a priori*, as he himself says, but he does in addition trace elements which, though preceding empirical language, nevertheless have content, as, for example, "man," "something," "one." If with him, therefore, the emphasis falls on elementary logical categories, with the logical positivists it falls rather on logical operations. The attempt is made here to reduce everything that has any degree of content, like class-concepts, to the logical operations by which they are constituted. For this reason the

Husserlian analyses often have a more ontological ring than those of the logical empiricists. It must here be said that the ontological question, that is, the question of the connection between logical meaning and extralinguistic reality, is raised also by logical positivistic thinkers, as when, for example, they develop a semantics. But this is a connection with empirical reality, while Husserl's doctrine of meanings suggests a concern with reality above and beyond the empirical, even though Husserl has expressly rejected every form of Platonic, or metaphysical-realistic interpretation of his doctrine.

The same issue arises in the two following points of confrontation. First, with respect to a fifth point of difference: intentionality. In the discussion of this term, as sometimes employed by logical positivists, their whole polemic against Husserl is set forth. For Husserl intentionality is the "directedness" of an act of consciousness towards a *"Gegenstand."* This German term is translated by Ryle as "accusative" in order to make clear that it is not here a question of an "object" in the sense of an entity. The intentional accusative qualifies the act, so that the logical structure of "consciousness" is always given as "consciousness of. . . ." (observation-of, memory-of, etc.). It should be clear once again from this short summary of our previous expositions that Husserl is not presenting us with a metaphysics or an ontology of the relations between natural human consciousness and a transcendental reality. He is giving a logical description of the structure of consciousness as such. Yet to the logical positivists his description still sounds far too ontological. For are we not to conclude from this that the meanings to which consciousness is directed are somehow *there*—even though we might hesitate to use the word "exist" in the everyday sense?

Accordingly, the logical positivist description of intentionality is wholly in line with their view of "meaning" as outlined above. Intentionality is for them *one* of the relations which can exist between concepts, as, for example, between "tree-experience" and "tree." Or, to word it differently, "intentional consciousness" is a description of a particular meaning of the word "to know," namely, in the sense of knowing that something is the case. These descriptions, the first in particular, have not been without difficulty, because a purely formal interpretation proved to be inadequate and the question was raised concerning the semantic status of words, especially in Carnap's descriptions. This is not to say, however, that we wish to adopt the Husserlian doctrine with its pure analysis of meanings, for this also leads to difficulties. When the intentionality of consciousness is assigned such a dominant role, meanings acquire a more independent status and can no longer be viewed as merely "a style of operations," as the way in which words are used within the logical rules.

The foregoing differences culminate in a sixth, namely, that concerning the independence of meanings. Husserl, as we have already observed, rejected every Platonic interpretation of meanings, since they were not to be thought of as belonging to a metaphysical realm of which empirical reality was a copy. Yet the difference with the logical empiricist description persists, and by comparison Husserl's arguments certainly give the impression of presenting a kind of metaphysics of self-existent meanings. For Husserl speaks, as previous chapters have shown, of "intuiting" ideal laws which constitute the logical essence of phenomena. Logical investigation has with him the character of discovery, which implies that there is something to be discovered. To be sure, this is not a metaphysical entity, something existing in a Platonic, transcendent space. We have already seen that Husserl rejects such a metaphysical "duplication" of reality, since it is not his intention to map out a plan of factual reality of a higher or lower order, but to investigate logical validity *beyond* human, empirical history, which he therefore refers to in terms like "*Sätze an sich*" (self-contained rules) and "eternal truths."

All this forms a sharp contrast with what is taught within the circle of neo-positivism, in all its phases of development. This division concerns more than the point now in question; it is rather a junction of dividing lines which run through the whole structure of these schools. Thus Husserl holds the view that the meaning of the simple name is fundamental and precedes predication, and thus precedes the meaning of a context, as he argues at length in his LOGICAL INVESTIGATIONS (vol. II, 1). Wittgenstein, on the other hand, says that only a proposition has meaning (or, in his own terminology, "sense,") and only within this context does a name acquire meaning. For both, meaning is connected with operations. For Husserl,

however, this operation involves a concentration, a fixing of attention—recall his use of the word "apperception," containing the idea
of a direction of mind toward something beyond itself. His conception of intentionality is connected with this; consciousness is consciousness of. . . . Logical positivism, as we have just observed,
speaks of "a style of operations," so that for Ryle the expression
"consciousness of . . ." does not refer to an "accusative," but refers
back to "consciousness" as a specific operation, one that has a certain
achievement and that can be better expressed as: knowing that
something is the case.

Where Husserl speaks of an elementary insight, in the logical
sense, the logical empiricists recognize only certain operations which
give rise to meanings. There are no eternal laws to which these
operations refer, nor any "thought" behind and apart from the
operations. Thus Ayer can give an operational definition of "thought"
as the manipulating of symbols in accordance with rules. Husserl,
incidentally, is not opposed to an operational approach, but con-
fines its validity to artificial languages, like that of arithmetic. He
speaks, moreover, of "the much loved comparison of arithmetical
operations with those of a game that is governed by rules," like
chess. He pursues the comparison further (wholly in line with the
logical empiricists here) by pointing out that the meaning which
the chess-men possess in the game does not depend on the material
of which they are made or the form which they have. It is the rules
of the game which give them their meaning. Now, arithmetical signs
also have a primitive meaning, which does not, however, enter into
arithmetic, for here their meaning is governed by the arithmetical
operations in accordance with established rules. Arithmetical signs
are thus less ambiguous; their meaning, derived entirely from the
"rules of the game," makes possible a flexible mode of procedure.

In Husserl's view an operational procedure of this kind has a more
limited validity. First, because he holds the view that it applies only
to systems which operate with exact symbols. Second, because he
accepts a more primitive meaning of signs and symbols prior to their
operational use—one could say, a less technical meaning, more
intuitive and natural. In his later studies on logic FORMAL AND
TRANSCENDENTAL LOGIC and EXPERIENCE AND JUDGMENT, these ideas

are worked out in detail. They are also connected with his later philosophy, where he sets geometry and physics against the background of the direct experience of the "life-world."

It appears that on this issue of "logical meaning," as on the other issues discussed here, they go their separate ways—even if one can only appreciate the extent of this separation by keeping in mind the many points of similarity both in method and intention. This can now be formulated more definitively. It can be stated that both schools wish to analyze the logical meaning of thought apart from circumstances of fact, which can be studied by sciences like psychology and neurology. Despite their holding this intention in common, a difference of view becomes very soon apparent. This can be expressed by saying that the phenomenological method conceives meaning in a more material sense, logical positivism in a more formal sense. The consequence of this difference in approach one can express, somewhat sharply, as follows: the Husserlian method makes logical operations dependent on meanings, while the logical positivist method makes meanings dependent on logical operations.

By this comparison the credit seems to go to the conception of logical positivism. Husserl gives the impression, in his views on eidetic reduction, evidence and the logical laws of essences, of requiring a trans-empirical experience. Logical knowledge is more than the classification of the elements of language in accordance with certain rules; there is a peculiar logical "insight." The elements of language, therefore, are also more than chess-men; they have meaning in themselves, not merely in terms of the logical rules within a certain methodology. This, for the logical positivists, is a sort of linguistic animism. Ryle and Ayer consider this primitive meaning, lodging in a word like a soul in a body, to be a myth. Wittgenstein too, even in his later period when his views on this point become modified, opposes the idea of "meanings" as mysterious entities hidden behind words. Moreover, Husserl accepts a trans-empirical experience, and he does so precisely because he distinguishes the meaning in entirely operational terms. For he believes it is possible to intuit essential meanings as given in concrete phenomena. Is there not a danger here of duplicating reality, even though Husserl denies this? And above all, how can one demonstrate intersubjectively that there are trans-empirical meanings which are *more* than what can be done with a particular word in accordance with the existing rules of language?

Now, as we have previously shown, Husserl has never taught an extreme realist doctrine of hidden meanings, which, like Platonic ideas, inhabit a trans-empirical world. He has referred time and again to experience in the logical sense, that is, to apperception, to "the concentration of attentiveness," to the process of identification, all of which take place in the forming of a proposition and which do not admit of factual, psychological description. Only in the logical process can one discover that what is in view in such a logical intention is never bound to facts, to contingent events, but possesses in itself a truth which is independent of fact and which can therefore be called absolute. Husserl's concern is not with *vérités de fait,* but with *vérités de raison.* But even if one recognizes this and is unwilling simply to brand Husserl's view as linguistic animism, the difficulty remains that Husserl has to posit a higher factual order of *Sätze an sich* (self-contained logical rules) if he is to safe-guard the logical investigation and detach it from an empirical basis. In so doing, has he not resolved the tension between the logical and the factual all too rashly by making the first independent and absolute?

This tension can be traced throughout the whole history of philosophy. It arises also in neo-positivist doctrines, even if, as we shall argue, it assumes another form. The classical solution was given by Leibniz, who formulated the distinction between *vérités de fait* and *vérités de raison,* and who is mentioned frequently by logical positivists and phenomenologists alike. Factual truths, according to Leibniz, concern that which can be established empirically, that which is at our disposal in the given world. Logical truths, on the other hand, are eternal, not bound to empirical facts and not only applicable to the given world, but necessary. Leibniz' metaphysics bridges over the tension between factual and logical truths. For what exists factually Leibniz introduces a new logical principle, that of sufficient reason. In his theodicy it appears that, according to this principle, factual existence is ultimately based on the goodness of God, who unites factual and logical truths in Himself, because in Him will and understanding, factual preference and logical priority, are one. Therefore, this factual, given world is "the best of all possible worlds."

Neither for phenomenologists nor for logical positivists can the chasm be bridged by metaphysics. The latter in general consider reasoning of this kind to be meaningless. Wittgenstein, however, holds the view that it is inexpressible. In his TRACTATUS he works out the idea that philosophy, and logic in particular, can only tell us *how* a thing is, never *what* it is. The world is then portrayed as a logical structure. *That* the world is Wittgenstein calls the inexpressible. Husserl, in a later work (FIRST PHILOSOPHY, vols. I and II), calls it an irrational fact that the world happens to exist; "every fact, and thus even the world-fact, is as fact . . . contingent." Husserl and Wittgenstein note the factor of probability which enters at the point where logical rules find a possible application to actual events. One could view this probability, which has come to figure largely in modern science and logic, as the non-metaphysical and more formalized equivalent of Leibniz' principle of sufficient reason.

However, this does not bridge the gap between logical and factual truths. For with Husserl logical meanings are something apart, closed to the influence of the factual world of history. Bar-Hillel, as we have seen, contests Husserl's view of independent meanings. He appreciates Husserl's intention of detaching the logical investigation of meanings from every empirical, or psychological, investigation. He points out, on the other hand, that the connection between logical analysis and the empirical sciences, such as psychology and sociology, must also be considered, and that up to the present time this problem has been unsolved. Husserl goes too far, especially in his earlier phase, in isolating logical truths from the empirically, contingently given, even if, by means of his intuiting of essences, he unveils the first by means of the second. But if, in his study of the essence of logical rules, he had taken more account of the impact of recalcitrant and contingent fact, it would have been apparent that logical "evidence" is less natural, less timeless, indeed less evident than Husserl supposed. The objections of the logical positivists to his doctrine of meaning and his concept of evidence point indeed to a tension that has been insufficiently worked out.

In another way, however, the attempt on the part of the logical positivists to solve the tension between the logical and the factual has also failed to meet with success. Here too there is an evident tendency to concentrate on a logically structured language that is withdrawn from the vicissitudes of empirical and historical life. Wittgenstein himself concludes his first major work, the TRACTATUS (where he judges a "logic of facts" to be impossible), with the idea that philosophy can only say what can be said, and thus can only comprise the propositions of natural science. To assert something about a particular logical network is to assert nothing about the world. But the fact that one can use one network better than another says something about the world. By formulating it in this way Wittgenstein obviously saw the empirical world more as nature than as the less rationally amenable world of history. Only in his later work does the historical world come more into the foreground, but then the network appears to have become less logical and more elastic, and even the tautologies, when related to historical life, become less "tautological," just as with Husserl "evidence" becomes less timeless.

This objection holds good even when there is no more talk of the conformity of language (logical network) with reality—as was still the case with, among others, Wittgenstein and Russell in about 1920 when they defended so-called "logical atomism": the elements of language were supposed to conform to the "atomic facts" of reality. One can relinquish this doctrine of conformity, deny what Wittgenstein affirmed in his TRACTATUS, that the meaning of a name is its object, and then define meanings wholly syntactically, i.e., in terms of their use within the context. But the objection applies then all the more forcibly that one has set up a doctrine of meanings that is divorced from the varying situations of life.

The first difficulty, then, is that a merely operational definition reduces the status of meaning to formal usage. Is a meaning no more than a particular use or application of a word? This question plays an important role in Wittgenstein's later work. Taking up certain formulations of Austin, Mohanty points out that there was a tendency among logical positivists to define meanings in terms of "capacity words," that is, in terms of what one can do with a word.

"I understand" a meaning was then reduced to: "I can" use this word in such and such a way. Similarly, these thinkers reduced categorical material-object statements (*e.g.*, "this book is red") to hypothetical sense-datum statements (*e.g.*, "one can have the perception of a red book."). In the later developments of linguistic analysis these reductions have been abandoned, for while statements of the first type ("I understand the meaning: 'this book is red'") imply statements of the second type, and may often be tested by them, they do not coincide in meaning.

This implies that Husserl's doctrine of meanings, even though liable to criticism, is an attempt to fill a gap which a purely operational definition leaves open. Further—for here is a second difficulty —the operations of language, however logically formalized, originate somewhere. One could try, for example, to establish operationally the meaning of "space" in the modern forms of mathematics. Then "space" would no longer mean what is generally called "space" in everyday language. But we cannot maintain with Carnap and Schlick, in the phase of their thought discussed in the last chapter, that formalized "space" has nothing to do with perceived space, but can be defined in entirely operational terms. On another point, that of intentionality, it has already become evident that a purely syntactic view of language, cut loose from its semantic implication, is impossible.

But here again the question arises of the connection of *vérités de raison* with *vérités de fait*, of a logical doctrine of meanings with the data of the empirical sciences, of clear, formalized structures with the contingent and often opaque facts of the historical and cultural situation in which men live and from which they derive their material. One may not, conversely, reduce the logical status of a meaning to these situations, for then one would fall prey again to psychologism—or to historicism, sociologism, etc.—which phenomenology and logical positivism so rightly opposed. But, on the other hand, men are evidently concerned with more than an unchangeable nature, or with purely objective and timeless linguistic structure, or with completely formalized operations emptied of historical significance. Logical truths never become wholly divorced from facts, even when the facts appear fickle and stubborn.

Objective language remains bound to the speaking subject and to his historical situations. We here touch the topics that are crucial to both schools of thought and that will occupy us in the following chapters.

Brief Bibliography

Y. Bar-Hillel, "Husserl's Conception of a Purely Logical Grammar," *Philosophy and Phenomenological Research,* vol. 17(1957).

G. Berger, "Husserl et Hume," *Revue internationale de Philosophie,* vol. 1(1939).

G. Bergmann, *The Metaphysics of Logical Positivism,* London, 1954.

B. Blanshard, *Reason and Analysis,* London, 1962.

R. Boehm, "Basic Reflection on Husserl's Phenomenological Reduction," *International Philosophical Quarterly,* vol. 5(1965).

F. Cowley, *A Critique of British Empiricism,* London, 1968.

H. Drüe, *Edmund Husserls System der phänomenologischen Psychology,* Berlin, 1963.

E. Fink, *Studien zur Phänomenologie* (1930-1939), The Hague, 1966.

F. Kaufmann, "Phenomenology and Logical Empiricism," *Essays in Memory of Edmund Husserl,* Cambridge, Mass., 1940. Reprinted, New York, 1968.

J. Kockelmans, *Edmund Husserl's Phenomenological Psychology,* Pittsburgh, Pa., 1967.

G. Küng, *Ontology and Linguistic Analysis,* tr. by E. Mays, Dordrecht, 1967.

J. Lyotard, *La Phénoménologie,* Paris, 1954.

H. Lübbe, "Das Ende des phänomenologischen Platonismus," *Tijdschrift v. Philosophie,* vol. 16(1954).

"Positivismus und Phänomenologie (Mach und Husserl)," *Beiträge zu Philosophie und Wissenschaft,* Munich, 1960.

G. Pedoli, *La fenomenologia di Husserl,* Turin, 1958.

G. Ryle, "The Theory of Meaning," *British Philosophy in Mid-century,* ed. by C. Mace, London, 1957.

H. Van Breda, ed., *Problèmes actuels de la Phénoménologie,* Paris, 1952.

Chapter Seven

The Phenomenology
of the "Ego"

"To the things themselves" (*Zu den Sachen selbst*) was an adage which Husserl advanced in various forms to characterize his method, and which became a signpost for thinkers of the phenomenological school. In Chapters Two and Three it became clear that this was in no sense a way of advocating that philosophy return to the things of daily experience. Husserl's interest lay in the disclosure of logically evident rules—even "thing" became a series of rules—while he wanted to remove questions of fact from the picture. Yet his studies seemed to a number of thinkers to present the possibility of constructing a realistic ontology on phenomenological foundations: Nicolai Hartmann, Moritz Geiger, Adolf Reinach and Hedwig Conrad-Martius made the attempt. But also in the various departments of philosophy and in relation to particular sciences the phenomenological method proved to be fruitful, as appears from the work of, among others, Roman Ingarden on art, Alfred Schütz on social science, Jean Héring and Gerard van der Leeuw on the phenomenology of religion. The eidetic reduction opened the way to the discovery of the universal essence in the concrete phenomenon, while the phenomenological reduction was frequently interpreted as an attitude completely free from prejudice.

Husserl's original intentions, however, had been more radical, for he had wanted a logical doctrine of method and not a science of facts. In his later development this became still clearer. The analysis of objective phenomena appeared then to refer back to the subject; Husserl drew up an "egology," a doctrine of the ego in its logical activity. It might be said that at this point the idealist phase of his philosophy set in, and indeed many of his more realist pupils would not go with him here. Curiously enough, it was precisely this transcendental idealism that brought about a closer confrontation between logical and factual truths, as a result of which he framed the doctrine of the life-world (*Lebenswelt*) where the factor of "history" dominated the factor of "nature." These latter elements led a subsequent generation of phenomenologists to adopt a realist ontology, which was, however, to center upon the human subject (thus taking up certain idealist elements from Husserl's doctrine), since the life-world was considered to be shaped by human existence. An example of this is to be found in the philosophy of Merleau-Ponty.

The concept of intentionality remains at the heart of Husserl's philosophy. It does not form a bridge between subject and object (as we saw in Chapter Two), for it is not described by Husserl as an ontological datum, but rather as a dynamic part of the logical mechanism, as when, for example, he points out how various acts (observation, fantasy, wish, etc.) can have the same intentional matter. Connected with this is the distinction between factual and logical data. The dynamic aspect of intentionality receives more and more attention in Husserl's later development. Intentionality is realized as a synthesis. The intentional object (an observed thing, an imagined event, a mathematical thesis, etc.) is not, it appears, the primary datum. Phenomenological analysis tries to penetrate further and discovers, as was indicated briefly at the end of Chapter Three, that every intentional datum comes into being as such, since it has to be conceived as a *particular* meaning (the house over there, continuing the same under varying perceptions; the event that acquired that particular meaning in imagination; the mathematical thesis viewed as such, rather than as a series of physical signs on paper, and so on). The isolated moments—perceptions, aspects, forms, etc.—are identified as a particular structure. This means that the intentional object is never simply given, but is effected within the intentionally directed attention, within the apperception, of consciousness. Husserl speaks of this structure of meaning as an achievement (*Leistung*) of the intentional activity of consciousness. Elsewhere he puts it as follows: there is here an overlapping of

different phases of consciousness, which, by this synthesis, constitutes the unity of an intentional object.

This latter formulation stems from a later period, from the PHE-
NOMENOLOGICAL PSYCHOLOGY of 1925, but the idea goes back as far
as 1905, when Husserl, in his THE PHENOMENOLOGY OF INTERNAL
TIME-CONSCIOUSNESS, clearly anticipated his later development by
analyzing time as a logical structure of the stream of consciousness.
This work is viewed by such authorities on Husserl as Fink, Landgrebe and Spiegelberg as the most significant for an understanding
of the dynamic and active function of intentionality, the more so that
it appeared so shortly after his LOGICAL INVESTIGATIONS. It becomes
clear from this how difficult it is to speak of chronological phases
in Husserl's thought; it is a case of shifting strata that are partially
overlapping. In any event, in his study on the consciousness of time,
he analyzes the construction of meanings (e.g., of "a continuing
object," "a note heard at a particular moment") from isolated
moments of time, which, by a synthetic activity of consciousness,
are made to overlap one another. Here, then, is the theme of that
phase of his thought that is usually located after 1913.

A large part of this analysis is devoted to the concept of "the
stream of consciousness." It figures again in the analyses of Carnap
(as outlined in Chapter Five), for Carnap's recourse to the stream
of experience, where distinctions as real-unreal have not yet been
made, shows a close resemblance to Husserl's bracketing of reality,
a resemblance noted by Carnap himself. However, this still belongs
to the first phase of the development of logical empiricism—at a
later stage Carnap had lost interest in the methodological reduction
to the stream of experience. But for Husserl it marked a new phase,
because, unlike Carnap, he considered this stream of experience as
centered in a subject, in a methodological "I" or "ego."

It is not our present purpose to trace the influences at work in the
"stream of consciousness" theme as handled by Husserl. In a sense,
the theme had already been considered by Augustine in connection
with his views on time. Without speaking in terms of a stream, Kant
referred to the isolation of elementary data (the "chaos of perceptions," Gewühl der Empfindungen) prior to their being unified by
"transcendental apperception." The British empiricists, to whom

Husserl makes frequent reference, developed the "stream of consciousness" theme; Berkeley wanted, as he said, to discover "rules" in the "continuous succession of ideas." In more recent times one may come across the theme in Brentano, William James and Henry Bergson, writers with whom Husserl was acquainted.

Husserl's intentions in the use of the term "stream of consciousness" will only be properly understood if seen as an attempt to describe the most primary data according to their logical structure. His concern, therefore, is not with a psychological analysis of internal experience, nor with a physical analysis of the phenomenon of time. Similarly, he renounces metaphysics of every possible form, whether it concerns a reality in the outside world or, on the contrary, one that is constructed in consciousness. Husserl wishes to define the structure which makes a particular phenomenon precisely what it is—"joy," "sound," "object," for example. As given phenomena, they must occupy a particular position and form in time (enduring, fleeting, etc.). Time is, as it were, the most general structure, but then one that is also continually on the move. Every moment is a new phase of time, and in virtue of this fact one is able to identify the specific form and position of a given phenomenon. Thus a permanent thing is like a stone in a clear pool: through the continual changes of the phases of time it shows itself identical in every new moment, in every new "now." In every "now" the preceding one is also contained; here again there is an identification in the overlapping of phases. Thus the enduring experience of joy is given as a continuum that occurs in a succession of interrelated phases of time: the experience-of-joy-now is qualified by its context, namely, as a continuation of the experience of joy of a moment ago, which in turn was related to the preceding phase. But even the sound that is now no longer heard is contained in the "now" as the sound-of-a-moment-ago, and echoes in the time-stream as the sound of an ever receding moment, so that successive identifications mark a specific position in the flow of time.

The elementary logical structure of every given phenomenon as a phenomenon in time is thus not to be understood passively, but as the result of a specific "directedness" of an active intentionality. This intentionality, according to Husserl, reaches out from every "now," to the past as well as to the future. In this way an over-lapping occurs by which fleeting and more lasting phenomena are identified, with their fixed position in time, and in virtue of which time, instead of crumbling into isolated moments, forms a continuous unity, comprising a variety of structures. This synthesizing intentionality occurs in the stream of consciousness, where "consciousness" has to be conceived, not as a real, psychological datum —this was pointed out at the end of Chapter Three—but as the elementary structure which Husserl calls the "constituting stream." He uses this term to indicate that every phase in which a "constitution" of time-structures occurs by way of the above-mentioned synthesis is a continuity in the perspective of every moment (*Abschattungskontinuität*). More simply, "consciousness" is understood here within the phenomenological reduction, and thus not as an actual datum.

Two important points in connection with these analyses remain to be mentioned. The first is what was cursorily referred to in the last chapter as the *vérités de fait* within the *vérités de raison*. Husserl attempts, as Carnap is to do many years later, to discover in the stream of consciousness an indisputable logical order, unaffected by the question of reality or unreality. What he discovers is a continuous progress of the moments of time, in which specific structures become apparent (a thing, a feeling of joy, etc.). But there is one purely factual datum that enters into this, and that cannot be explained away, even in terms of the effect of intentionality. It is the fact that the progress of time has a given, un-changeable tempo. In the structure thus logically analyzed Husserl discovers, in spite of himself, the shadow of fact; he then writes that this "change is somewhat absurd—that it should run its course precisely as it does, and can be neither faster nor slower."

A second important point, raised with some emphasis by Husserl, is the reference to subjectivity, which is to figure more largely in his later work. For Husserl speaks not only of the stream of time, but also of stream of consciousness. Why "consciousness," if it is only a question of the constitution of the structures of phenomena, and not of the actual psychological consciousness? This is connected with the position occupied by the "now" in the stream of time.

Intentionality operates from every present. In the "now" lies the moment of immediate experience. Husserl speaks of "experience of the present" (*Aktualitätserlebnis*) and of the "ultimate source" (*Urquellpunkt*); we are to see the image of the stream, then, as pointing to the fact that time has its source in the actual "now." Or, as Husserl analyzes it more precisely, every object can only be looked at, can be viewed *as* object, from a point of observation, from a "now." The stream of time, then, springing as it does from the "now," is not itself an objective datum, but a condition of objectification. Properly speaking, it is only with reference to the objective structures which are constituted in the stream of time that one can use the image of a "stream"; but this stream "is nothing 'objective' given in time. It is absolute subjectivity." The word "consciousness" thus acquires with Husserl the meaning, not only of that which is given directly, as later with Carnap, but also of that which is itself no more to be objectified, since it precedes objectivity and is in this sense subjectivity. This subjectivity becomes more central in te later thought of Husserl, where, as will appear, the *vérités de fait* are to break through the purely phenomenological, non-empirical construction of the subject.

In the second edition of LOGICAL INVESTIGATIONS (1913) his conceptual apparatus appears to be somewhat revised. He is now critical of the term that he himself used in the first edition, "self-contained truth" (*Wahrheit an sich*), which he considers to be too heavily weighted in favor of the *vérités de raison*. It is not that he wishes to intersect the field of logical and phenomenological research with *vérités de fait*, but that he now conceives the rules or truths discovered as related to the activity of the ego and its intentionality, rather than as given in themselves. The objections to the idea of a "pure I" (that is, of a logical construction on the part of the subject), which he raised in the first edition for fear of any form of "I-metaphysics," he now withdraws.

The one stream of time, which is reflected in all its phases, has both continuity and identity. The identity occurs in the "now" as the actual point at which plurality and unity, moments and their overlapping, come into being. Husserl speaks also of the "flowing present." This is, at the same time, the identity of the "I," which directs itself to the series of phenomena and wich is active in its attentiveness and effort, in apperception and logical synthesis. It becomes clearer that what is given in a variety of forms (lasting and fleeting, in observation or in memory, as a material object or a conceived thesis, etc.) becomes the mirror for the dynamic process of synthesis, which refers back to the activity of the subject. And this is not merely the theoretical subject, or the subject of observation; the identity of this subject carries with it the possibility of the subject's making a certain identification—of identifying, for example, the sounds heard at a concert with a piece of music heard in the past and now made present in memory. Thus part of the structure of the ego is the "I can," because the field of realizable possibilities lies within the capacity of the ego. Here again, it is not a question of what psychologically possible in a real or factual consciousness, but of what is logically contained in the subject's possibilities of identification.

This concept of "I can" is already to be found in his IDEAS, and more conspicuously in his FIRST PHILOSOPHY and PHENOMENOLOGICAL PSYCHOLOGY in connection with the transcendent character of the objective world. By this last idea Husserl means that the reality of, say, a perceived table is made evident by the fact that the table is never, in its meaning and as what is intentionally held in view, exhausted in the observation one has of it at a particular moment. In what at this moment I apprehend of the table which I see before me I discover at the same time something more: I do not conceive my perception as the table itself, nor as an exhaustive perception of the table, but as a particular perspective (*Abschattung*) in which I see the table. In my perceiving I know that I can apprehend more of the table, by looking at it, for example, from another side, or by walking toward it and touching it. The "I can" is given together with the momentary perception, makes it an aspect of perception (*Abschattung*) and thus shows that in the immanence of perception there lies the logical possibility of transcending it. So Husserl can speak of transcendence in immanence, not, of course, in a metaphysical sense, but as a structural qualification. That a given object is known to be real arises from the obvious fact that the object is not exhausted in its momentary perception. Husserl rejects Hume's doctrine on this point, since Hume would contend that the object consists entirely in the sense-data composing it. For the phenomenological method there is a horizon of possibilities which is essential for the determination of what is given. It becomes evident later that a number of philosophers in contemporary analytical philosophy reject the doctrine of sense-data on grounds very similar to those just mentioned.

A further illustration of the preceding discussion is offered by some of the more recent developments of the notion "I can." Stuart Hampshire offers us an analytical approach. He makes a distinction between the thing itself and its appearance within a particular situation to the perceiver. There are two ways of speaking corresponding to this: a thing "is this or that" and "it appears to me in this way." The last-named way of speaking makes uses of the language of sense-data, the language of perception; it should not be conceived, however, as dealing with "data," but with possibilities of reaching the thing itself. The distant tower appears to me to be round, but when I get close I see that it is octagonal. So-called sense-data should not be conceived as isolated little descriptions, but as forming part of the activities of a subject who tries to investigate an object. Hampshire's work bears the significant title THOUGHT AND ACTION: the "pieces" of perceiving and thinking are interpreted from the wider horizon of action, of the "I can."

A similar tendency can be seen in the philosophy of Maurice Merleau-Ponty, a phenomenologist who owes much to Husserl but also to more voluntaristic phenomenologists, such as Scheler. The human subject, says Merleau-Ponty, exists primarily as bodiliness and not as pure thought. That's why perception offers us ways of approaching an object. The object is apprehended in profiles, aspects, and these refer to ever new and further possibilities of investigating the surrounding world. Strictly speaking, considerations of this kind are already implied in Husserl's use of the expression "I can." In Husserl, however, the connection with the practical acting of the human subject is less directly given than in Hampshire or Merleau-Ponty. Husserl's "I can" has a more logical character; it indicates the possibilities of analyzing. On the other hand, Husserl's "I can" also is closely connected with the idea that every perceived object must be analyzed within its broader horizon. This concept of horizon was already implied in William James's term "fringe"—an idea which probably influenced Husserl and which plays a central role in the analysis of the field of perception by Husserl's disciple Aron Gurwitsch.

Husserl's doctrine of the horizon as a structure of phenomena figures largely in his later thought. The analyses we have outlined here he had already begun to work on in the period from 1905 to 1913. We could describe the development more generally by saying that his interest moved from an analysis of a single datum of perception to an analysis of the whole course of perception. His interest in the problems of time is connected with this. Here he is concerned with what perceptions imply, that is to say, with making logically explicit something that is not given directly. We always perceive more than is given to our retina—thus the much-used adage of phenomenology. In every observation there is, besides the element of "further possibilities," the element of a "fulfillment of directedness." In this way continuity can be broken and identifying intentionality can fall short, so that an oasis can turn out to be a mirage. But if certain continuous rules become apparent in the field of intentional activity, then the meaning of a certain phenomenon is constituted (e.g., "the house over there"). Husserl's dynamic conception of the mechanism of intentionality explains now why he cannot hold to a sense-data doctrine. He recognizes the existence of these perceptions, but calls them "hyletic data" or "sensory material," since they are taken up within the formative function of intentionality.

One discovers this formative element in the mirror of the object, which is conceived as this or that specific datum. In other words, one discovers it if one notices how consciousness is actively directed toward something, is consciousness of something (for example, of the table as a real object, not exhausted in the momentary perception). This formative moment Husserl calls the "noetic moment" or "noesis." This is the "consciousness" that constitutes unity, identity, in the multiplicity of its phases (stream of consciousness, the *Abschattungen* of observations, etc.). Corresponding to this at the anti-pole is the "noema," that is, the one object, the permanent pole, which becomes evident in the multiplicity of the phases of consciousness.

A striking feature is the unity of the subjective and objective poles, a unity which is not first established by a phenomenological analysis, but is found to be the presupposition of every distinction between subject and object. The "I can," as we have said, belongs essentially to the ego, and this was found to imply that every datum of perception is conceived within much wider horizons, which in their continuity display certain rules. It appeared, in connection with this, that the correlation of "noesis" and "noema" occurs within the dynamics of the stream of consciousness with its identifying syntheses. The reality-status of the world was seen to rest, therefore, not on perceptions, on "hyletic" data, but on a formative intentionality. This transcendence in immanence thus pointed to the activity of the ego. This ego, considered as the purely subjective pole, is then the correlate of the whole, ever-widening field of time, that is, of the stream of time with its phases of consciousness and the dimensions of present, past and future. Certain rules and structures become evident here, as, for example, in apprehending an event, with its fixed place in time, in the "following" consciousness of time, rules by which this field is defined and by which consciousness or the ego can be directed intentionally toward particular, identifiable data. But, then, these data are given within the illimitable perspectives of the "I can," or, as Husserl also puts it, within the infinity of the process.

All this can be summarized more simply by saying that part of the meaning of given reality is that it is unlimited: every real datum is apprehended in perspective, so that one can speak of "transcendence" in "immanence," since a datum, on every occasion it is perceived in one way or another, is conceived as something more than is actually given in that phase of consciousness. But this unlimitedness of reality is precisely what does not occur in perceptions or in sense-data; it belongs to the intentional activity of the ego as the subjective pole of the field of consciousness. Thus the unlimitedness of reality falls back on "consciousness," and although Husserl clearly does not intend to present here a metaphysical idealism, but rather to analyze the logical structures of meaning, this may be called a methodological—Husserl himself calls it a transcendental—idealism.

The part played by the transcendental ego in Husserl's philosophy may be clarified in the light of the identifications that can be made in another direction. Further, one must focus one's view on the subjective, and no longer on the objective, pole. To do this, we may take the example of perceiving a table. Here consciousness is directed "straight at" the object. But now it may bend back upon itself in reflection. It is then directed not on the object observed but on the subject that observes. Before, the ego or subject was hidden, as it were, in the intentionality of the perception. Now it is made explicit. Initially, according to Husserl the ego functions anonymously. But some further thought will show that, even when attention is turned explicitly to the subject of perception, an anonymous ego is still to be found, the subject of reflection. In saying this, however, we have named the anonymous and so regressed along the line of self-reflection. Just as in the analysis of the objective world we find an unlimitedness—the *"etcetera"* belongs to the essence of "thing," says Husserl—so in this subjective dimension there appears in the same way an infinity—the *"ad infinitum"* belongs to the essence of the self-reflection of the ego. In neither case is it a question of physical or psychological infinity. It is the structure of infinity that here becomes apparent.

In the subjective dimension also there occurs a process of continual identification, which is the more remarkable in that it always points to the same subjective pole. In the objective world there were found to be innumerable forms of identification; that of the perceived tree is different from that of the perceived piece of music, and this is different again from that of the comprehended theorem, and so on. To be sure, this broad and boundless field of phenomena found its ultimate form of unity in the structure of time, since something is known to be real if it can be located in time. This time-structure was connected with the ever present "now," that is to say, it points to the presence of the ego as the point from which the co-ordinates of time are placed.

This identification of the ego receives more emphasis if one notes the various acts in which reflection takes place. I listen to a concert that I have heard once before. I can then reflect on the ego of some years back that was present at the concert then given. I can also reflect on the ego that was thinking at the time of its own activity of listening. Here too one can see an infinite series of levels of reflections, while the ego identified is the same throughout. Husserl speaks of the structural possibilities of recurring again and again to oneself, and he calls these "reiterations." It is by way of these reiterations that the self-identification of the ego takes place. But here the anonymous ego is still at work, the subject enacting the self-identification. This ultimate subjective pole is absolute subjectivity, in the sense that it can never be made the object of reflection, but can only be discerned indirectly as the hidden source in the series of reiterations, the self-identifications.

A few important points remain to be made. First, the agreement of this with what Husserl discussed much earlier in his study on time-consciousness, where he maintains that one can speak of the stream of time only in connection with the objective structures that were constituted in it, whereas the "stream" itself is not given in time, is not objective, but forms the condition of this. In his early study, discussed at the beginning of this chapter, Husserl writes: "for all this we lack names." From his later analyses of the ego this becomes even clearer: there remains always a subjective pole, an operational "I," an anonymous ego. Here Husserl discovers a structure—more than this one may not say, for one is not concerned here with something that exists, something given in time, that can be located and named. In these terms in fact this structure proves to be unnameable and thus to fall outside the bounds of language, but is not itself within their scope. On the other hand, the ego requires locatable data and even its own, objectifying self-identifications in order to be itself, that is, in order to act as an operational "I," an anonymous ego.

In his last writing Husserl was still wrestling with this problem of the relation of the anonymous ego to the phenomenological self-reflection of the ego. He made the attempt again and again, sometime briefly in notes, to eliminate the refractoriness of this final datum—though the word "datum" can hardly be used here, because this already presupposes an identification in time and thus an intentionality of the ego. Remarkable here is the fact that we have on the one hand an avowed transcendental idealist structure, and on the other hand something that proves to be irreducible and is in this sense "factual." Husserl's attempts were idealist in the sense that he sought a deeper, "passive" self-constitution of this anonymous ego.

A further point, connected with this, is that this unnameable ego-pole may in no respect be equated with the concrete "I" of living, historical men. Least of all does Husserl give a biography, or even a psychology. Everything human, including the human "I," is objectified by this ego. This leads once again to the tension we spoke of before. Now it means this. Husserl must acknowledge on the one hand that this transcendental ego has nothing human left to it, is entirely "solitary," and that only in an equivocal sense it can be called "I"; and on the other hand that this ego can manifest itself only as the concrete person performs the phenomenological self-reflection, and thus (in a certain sense, necessarily) as the ego acts as a man in the world. But this raises the question, acutely, of the relation of the phenomenological structure, the anonymous ego (*vérité de raison*), to the historical structure, the human person (*vérité de fait*). So Husserl writes in his CRISIS that the ego is given apodictically, but that it "must be brought to expression." But this, he says, raises the issue of the concrete world, of the phenomenological meaning of "society," "person," "history," "birth" and "death."

Brief Bibliography

H. U. Asemissen, "Strukturanalytische Probleme der Wahrnehmung in der Phänomenologie Husserls," *Kantstudien*, Erg. Heft, 73, Cologne, 1957.
———, "Egological Reflexionen," *Kantstudien*, 1959.

W. Biemel, "Die entscheidenden Phasen der Entfaltung von Husserls Philosophie," *Zeitschrift f. philos. Forschung,* vol. 13(1950).

G. Brandt, *Welt, Ich und Zeit,* The Hague, 1955.

G. Eigler, *Metaphysiche Voraussetzungen in Husserls Zeitana-lysen,* Meisenheim, 1961.

A. Gurwitsch, *Field of Consciousness,* Pittsburgh, 1964.

K. Held, *Lebendige Gegenwart. Die Seinsweise des transzend-entalen Ich bei Husserl,* The Hague, 1966.

E. Husserl, *Cartesian Meditations,* tr. by D. Cairns, The Hague, 1960.

————, *The Paris Lectures,* tr. by P. Koestenbaum, The Hague, 1964.

————, *Ideen zu einer reinen Phänomenologie und phänome-nologische Philosophie,* vols. 2 and 3, ed. by M. Biemel, The Hague, 1952.

————, *Erste Philosophie,* vols. 1 and 2(1923-24), ed. by R. Boehm, The Hague, 1956 and 1959.

————, *Phänomenologische Psychologie* (1925), ed. by W. Biemel, The Hague, 1962.

————, *Analysen zur passiven Synthesis* (1918-26), ed. by M. Fleischer, The Hague, 1966.

I. Kern, *Husserl und Kant,* The Hague, 1964.

J. Kockelmans, ed., *Phenomenology: The Philosophy of Edmund Husserl and Its Interpretation,* Garden City, N.Y., 1967.

H. Kuhn, "The Phenomenological Concept of 'Horizon,'" *Essays in Memory of Edmund Husserl,* ed. by M. Farber, Cambridge, Mass., 1940.

P. Ricoeur, *Husserl. An Analysis of His Phenomenology,* tr. by E. Ballard and L. Embree, Evanston, Ill., 1967.

Chapter Eight

The Phenomenology of the Life-World

IN THE final phase of his phenomenological research Husserl focused his attention on the field of human history, and specifically by introducing the theme of the "life-world" (*Lebenswelt* or *Lebensumwelt*). This "life-world" appears at first blush to be a reference to the reality of immediate experience. But in fact this too refers to the perspective of the transcendental egology. Husserl had to turn to the world of facts and history in order to explain how even here the ego secretly operates, and how concrete historical structures are logically necessary, rather than contingent, as a process by which the anonymous ego acquires a name. Here was the field of investigation where the methodical idealism of Husserl was to culminate in the clarification of fact (*vérités de fait*) in terms of the rules of reason (*vérités de raison*), understood as a limitless process of "achievement" by the operational ego.

This purpose was never fulfilled. Clearly, the life-world is not to be conceived in a realistic manner, nor as a particular concept of culture. The concept of the "life-world" was from the outset comprehended within the phenomenological reduction. But fact in its ultimate, transcendental necessity could not be explained in this way. Problems about the world of culture and history, about historical values, the nature of the physical, and intersubjectivity only led to a more acute tension between the purely "abstract" and "solitary" egological dimension on the one hand and the variegated historical and social "world-dimension" of phenomenological philosophy on the other. In the remainder of this chapter we shall explain this more fully.

Two things need to be added here. First, that Husserl clearly continues the line that was sketched in the previous chapter, namely, the disclosure of "transcendence" in "immanence." This was evident in both his analysis of the world (*e.g.*, by way of the implications of perception) and his analysis of self-reflection and its reiterations. Ultimately it is a question of one transcendence—the transcendental ego—in all immanence. This line is now continued into the life-world, so that his analyses are not simply social or anthropological studies.

Now it is precisely this tension with the historical world that gives such a notable turn to his thought—and this is the second point that needs to be made. Husserl investigates the history of human thought according to the various forms which this has assumed. The tradition of Greek thought, maintained in the culture of Europe, he finds to be characterized by "idealization," that is to say, by tracing at the level of "the boundless" the rules that govern concrete phenomena. The mathematical formalization of nature is an illustration of this. The "infinity" that emerges is formalized in logical and mathematical terms and is evidence of the activity of human reason. And "reason" itself as a concept and as an ideal was a product of Greece. Now, this points to the fact that within the perspective of history "transcendence in immanence" has assumed a certain structure, the ideal of the self-reflection of reason, an ideal that has become prominent in European culture. Husserl is concerned with actual history, and that not as an inevitable process, but as history that embodies a task, a duty, and that as such depends on the human response. Accordingly, his analyses develop into moral exhortation and reflection. He does not speak now merely in the language of logical analysis or of "constatives," but also in the language of praxis and of "performatives" and commands. So, at the point where he is unable to give a definitive explanation of history in terms of the activity of the ego, his philosophy acquires a certain pathos.

The phenomenology of Husserl here shows an affinity with existentialism, though, in seeing this, one must not overlook the points of dispute. The position that Husserl adopts in POSTSCRIPTS TO THE "IDEAS" (*Nachwort zu den Ideen*, 1930), over against the philosophy of his former pupil Heidegger is this, that a philosophy of concrete "existence," like that of associated metaphysical problems, is blind to the originality of the phenomenological reduction, the intention of which is to penetrate the factual, "mundane" existence of man so as to reach the transcendental subjectivity. He held this position to his latest development. Existentialism arose partly from impulses of an entirely different source, such as the religious thought of Kierkegaard, and partly from phenomenology. Thinkers such as Heidegger (the relation of existence and time to the "world"), Jaspers (a phenomenological analysis of states of consciousness and of attitudes to life) and Sartre (an analysis of the correlation of consciousness, freedom and world) can in some respects be viewed as phenomenologists. The later development of Husserl, however, presents still more points of contact, especially in the theme of the life-world that is further developed by Merleau-Ponty with a more existentialist tone.

The theme of the life-world is closely connected with the analysis of the horizon mentioned earlier. Husserl speaks of a given world-horizon as the environment of every phenomenon, a horizon to which every phenomenon implicitly refers. He compares this doctrine himself with William James's doctrine of the "fringe" that surrounds each phenomenon, but at the same time points out that James does not then make a methodical enquiry into the implications, the hidden dynamic processes within this horizon-structure. It is Husserl's express intention, especially where the horizon of the life-world is concerned, "to free the consciousness of the world from its anonymity," and thus to offer a transcendental—more then than a factual, descriptive—analysis. In this he goes beyond the analysis of a particular pattern of culture as an empirical life-world, an analysis such as Lévy-Brühl gives in his studies on the primitive world, to which, as it happens, Husserl owes much for his own doctrine of the life-world.

Primitive man lives in the world of myth. The time-structure of this world is that of an ever-flowing present and in the strict sense is not yet historical. Modern man lives in a historical world, which means that his world is everywhere changed. Now man can free himself from the immediate sphere of interest and turn to investi-

gate the world as a whole. This happened for the first time in
Greece, where they thought it the duty of reason to comprehend
the world, and where everyday facts (a boundary between pieces
of land, a round object, etc.) were formalized and thought through
to the level of the infinite (a straight line, a circle, etc.). From a
phenomenological point of view, there is a certain inevitability in
this factual historical development, because in this way the infinite
dimension of the activity of reason becomes visible within the life-
world. There is a theoretical disclosure of finite things and of
limited human action (praxis); transcendence is set free within
immanence. The analysis of the life-world becomes a comprehensive
vision of the world as a whole, which Husserl compares with the
insight into a complicated organism that can only be acquired by
going beyond mere explanation to a view of it in terms of the
life that is in it and that makes it what it is. Elsewhere Husserl
describes the ego as a life impulse.

It is within this framework that one must see Husserl's discussions on the rise of the natural sciences. He rejects the idea that the
natural sciences describe a self-contained physical objectivity, hidden behind our subjectively colored life-world. For these sciences
themselves arose by an idealization of patterns from the everyday
world; they were founded on inductions which, as an expression of
practical control and prediction, were determined themselves by
everyday life. It was a question of finding the most appropriate
yardsticks that science could apply to the life-world. In the unend-
ing progress of its method science makes a "coat of ideas" to fit
the life-world as nearly as possible. In contrast to this, Husserl
himself views logical and mathematical objectivity as an expression of the activity of human consciousness and its transcendental
function within the life-world. He continues to recognize with
Bolzano the existence of such things as self-contained propositions
(*Sätze an sich*) and self-contained truth (*Wahrheit an sich*), but
now as related to human activity and so as sharing in the culture
of the concrete life-world.

Thus behind every logical judgment there lies a pre-predicative
experience which is part of the structure of the life-world and which
alone makes this judgment possible. The idea of an "absolute"

truth is rejected here. Not that truth is only relative; but it has a "horizon," which represents the scope of the (originally hidden) activities of the practical subject. Even the market-dealer, according to Husserl in his FORMAL AND TRANSCENDENTAL LOGIC (1929), has his market-truth with an appropriate "relativity," namely, that which is better or worse in market-practice.

Husserl, in this way, makes the logical truths (*vérités de raison*) relational, that is to say, related to the forms of human life. His research has in view the disclosure of the ego's constructive activity in the world of human culture as a whole, but leads only to a clearer view of the impact of concrete and historical forms of life on the rational and logical structures. This needs now to be elaborated with respect to three themes: history, corporality and intersubjectivity. We shall then devote some attention to other phenomenological thinkers who have developed these themes.

The phenomenological doctrine of the life-world is that the primary existents are not physical objects, sober facts and scientific laws (natural laws), but value-objects such as paintings, houses, articles of use, even practical dealings and expectations, in short, "the world of praxis, beauty, values, grief, care, and so forth . . . as a world that derives meaning from communicative experience . . . ," says Husserl in the second volume of his FIRST PHILOSOPHY. He speaks there also of the unity of the "infinite coherence of life in the infinity of the intersubjective, historical life to which it belongs." This raises the question of history, which Husserl calls the science (*Wissenschaft*) of personal facticity which is at the same time universally conceived (in PHENOMENOLOGICAL PSYCHOLOGY, 1925). This theme was never developed to the full by Husserl. Yet it indicates clearly the remarkable tension in his thought, occasioned by the pressure of facticity. What we have referred to previously in terms of the *vérités de fait*, thus recalling the oldest debates of philosophy and, in particular, the contribution of Leibniz, is brought forcibly to the fore once again. All possible structures of the world are traced within the broad field of the logical operations of the ego, but then the fact of history, the irreducible datum of the historical existence of this particular world, remains a recalcitrant fact. We mentioned in this connection at the end of Chapter Six the statement of Husserl to the effect that the "fact of the world" as fact is contingent. That the world in fact exists is a point beyond which we cannot go; it is a "transcendental fact." That of the countless logically possible worlds and forms of consciousness *this* world and *this* consciousness factually exist, and indeed, that logical rules as such find a field of application in a factual nature, all this is an irreducible fact that falls outside the scope of phenomenology and logic and that may, in this sense, be said to belong to metaphysics, according to Husserl.

Now, we may observe in isolated remarks a significant turn in Husserl. With his view turned to history and society he no longer regards this factual existence as the one instance, the specific illustration, of the many logical possibilities open to the operations of the ego, but conversely, he regards the transcendental analyses only as a means that must be made subservient to the *vérités de fait,* to the natural world and its forms of life. "Our interest lies therefore in the factual. In wider perspective, transcendental phenomenology is a tool for the transcendental science of facts." At this point he even speaks of the "calling" of phenomenology to interpret the true meaning of the natural, given world.

"Corporality" forms a second theme in Husserl, which points in the same way toward factual and contingent existence. From his lengthy discussions in IDEAS (vols. II and III) and PHENOMENOLOGICAL PSYCHOLOGY we can note the following points. When the world is perceived in immediate experience, prior to its being objectified in science, things appear in certain perspectives; one sees, for example, the front of a house, but not the back. These perspectives refer back to the spatially limited position of the body of the observer in question. In every field of perception—however much this may later become generalized and formalized by science— there is a kind of scheme of co-ordinates in which the body of the person occupies the reference point of zero. An analysis of movement, reminiscent in some ways of Berkeley's discussions in DE MOTU, shows that every ascertainment of movement presupposes the "resting-point" of the observer. One's orientation in the world displays rules that are related to one's own corporality. Moreover, the field of the "I can," of kinaesthetic experiences, belongs essentially to the structure of the body.

All this lies prior to the objectification of the "I" as a thing among things. When this takes place one is inclined to conceive the living "directedness" of the body as a "soul" in the sense of something that is added to it. By the word "soul," in fact, one is indicating certain rules according to which the body moves and behaves toward others. Viewed as subject, that is, as a center for possible orientation, the body is experienced as directly animated, so that the soul does not form a kind of special layer on the structure of the body. One cannot locate the soul—one cannot say, for example, that thought is actually *in* the head—for it is a case of intentional experience: physically conditioned perceptions (also called by Husserl "hyletic") are taken up in references to something else. Man becomes a person by this "animation" of his physical nature, by which also body and soul are given in one. This becomes evident in another respect in the objects of culture that man has produced. When, for example, an arrow is cut, we have to begin with a physical object, perceptible purely by the senses, but we have at the same time the intention that is expressed in the word "arrow" and that is connected with the directed attention of the person who made the arrow, as well as with his cultural world.

In these analyses Husserl rejects the "naturalist" conception of the human body as an object among objects, and develops a "personalist" conception in which the unity of body and soul is prominent, and where materialist and behaviorist ideas as well as a doctrine of layers (*Schichten*) in man are discarded. Moreover, he tries to show that the facticity, the contingency, that human corporality obviously has, is structurally necessary. Ultimately, his analyses show body and soul as one phenomenon with its structure determined by the ego.

Closely connected with this are Husserl's comprehensive discussions on the existence of other minds, on intersubjectivity. This problem caused Husserl considerable trouble: does not his phenomenology imply, as he himself said and as was in fact the case with Carnap's philosophy, a methodical solipsism, a perfect "solitariness" of the ego? It must be obvious at this point once again that the transcendental phenomenological reduction is a methodical mechanism of a highly complicated nature, and that, to be of use, it has constantly to be renewed. It must never be supposed that it has fathomed at last the ultimate depths.

There are two phenomena in the world of immediate experience that point unmistakably toward intersubjectivity—Husserl was never a solipsist. The first is the above-mentioned corporality. The knowledge one has of one's body is attained together with the experience of the bodies of other people as animated bodies. Second, the objectivity of the world or of a particular thing also reflects this intersubjectivity. One of the logical characteristics of an object that is given in direct relation to me as an observer is that it is not dependent on me, but can also be observed by others. Here objectivity is the correlate of intersubjectivity.

How then is the other person conceived as another subject, as an *alter ego?* This question carries us back to intentionality, which operates in such a way as to conceive a datum outside me as, at the same time, another mind. In the conclusion of his CARTESIAN MEDITATIONS Husserl has offered a solution that is in many respects reminiscent of the monadology of Leibniz. Here Husserl denies emphatically that he is giving a metaphysical construction or appealing to a kind of intuition by which one may learn of other minds. No, it is a question of methodical necessity that, in one's own subjectivity, the meaning of *alter ego* should show itself. Essential to the structure of the ego is that it finds itself in its own "present," as the actual source of the stream of time, and that at this point there appears at the same time the presence of other irreducible sources, points where a "now" is also apparent. This Husserl calls "appresentation," positing the other as present. He also employs the term "empathy" (*Einfühlung*) for this, which is not, however, an instance of psychological intuition, as understood by psychologists in their description of the source of the knowledge of the other, but a case of a directly given structure of transcendence, of the other "I" in one's own "I," of intersubjectivity in subjectivity. This forms in its turn the foundation for the objectivity of the given world. In view of the fact that this is a structure Husserl can speak of "transcendental intersubjectivity," and when he calls the methodically isolated "I" a "monad," in which the presence of other monads is reflected, even then he is not talking about a metaphysics of substances, but giving a methodological characterization of intentional operations. In his later work, CRISIS, this transcendental intersubjectivity is still further reduced to the activity of the "solitary" ego. But then the problems we have mentioned about "contingent fact" at once re-emerge, for he sees at the same time the necessity of the ego acting, by way of intersubjectivity (in the transcendental sense, but also in a real and tangible form), in the historical context of human society.

In 1927 Heidegger had published his BEING AND TIME in the journal for phenomenological research edited by Husserl. It was a phenomenological analysis of human subjectivity, in which, however, he rejected the idea of the ego as an impartial onlooker, and moved toward the idea of a perspective not issuing from the subject, the perspective of "Being." In 1936/37 Jean-Paul Sartre published an article in which he explicitly criticized Husserl's concept of the transcendental ego. Sartre saw here an idealist tendency in so far as Husserl attributed to the ego a special priority, divorcing it from, and indeed contrasting it to, the phenomena of immediate experience. Sartre himself developed a phenomenology in which the subject, "consciousness," is not primarily reflective, but intentional, that is to say, in continual directedness to something outside itself. He elaborated this basic idea in analyses of the concrete phenomena of life, in connection with the theme of human freedom.

The trend in more recent French philosophy known as existentialism has in general been influenced by Husserl's phenomenology. One may trace this influence to some extent in Gabriel Marcel and Jean Wahl, more noticeably in Jean-Paul Sartre, Maurice Merleau-Ponty, Paul Ricoeur and Emmanuel Levinas. Here, more than in German existentialism, human corporality becomes the subject of phenomenological research. Marcel referred at an early stage to the dimension of subjectivity in which the body is apprehended— "I am my body"—in distinction from the dimension of objectivity— "I have my body." Sartre defines the structure of the body as the necessity of factual contingency; that is to say, rather than analyze a general logical structure, he wants to derive the necessity (*vérité de raison*) from the facticity which is given in the human body with its field of possibilities ("I can"—freedom) and which cannot be reduced. It was this that led his critics to regard his philosophy as psychology and factual description. Essential also to this factual structure is intersubjectivity. And this, again, not as a logical or transcendental structure, but as given in the view by which my own self-consciousness is formed, for this view of the other can justify or condemn me; thus from the beginning it is involved in my self-reflection and self-knowledge.

The phenomenological philosophy of Merleau-Ponty, influenced partly by Sartre, is dominated by the theme of corporality, a theme that is closely related to the Husserlian theme of the lived world, which he had studied in Husserl's manuscripts before these were published in the 1950s. He sees at the center of Husserl's later research the implicit operations of intentionality as these are at work in pre-theoretical, pre-predicative experience. An attempt is here made to bring to light the unity of the subject and its world, for it appears that the structure of, and the things in, the world are not given merely objectively, but refer precisely to the intentional activity of the subject. It is significant, on the other hand, that the completion of Husserl's reduction proves to be impossible, according to Merleau-Ponty. This points to the fact that there cannot be an absolute ego, and that, consequently, the true phenomenological reduction is that which leads, in Heidegger's words, to "being-in-the-world."

Merleau-Ponty's philosophy as a whole is an elaboration of these fundamental theses. Behind the world of objects, of natural laws and logical concepts, a world that arises by the objectifying activity of language and science, phenomenological analysis discloses the ambiguous, pre-objective world of immediately lived experience, *expérience vécue*. Here man and world, inner world and outer world, the spiritual and the material are given only in mutual interlacement. Consequently, the phenomenological reduction for Merleau-Ponty is neither transcendental not logical; it is a bracketing of the objectified world of the sciences, purified of all ambiguity. One can then have a clear view of the world of immediate perception, where reality is given in direct correlation with one's own subjective corporality. Merleau-Ponty's major work is called PHENOMENOLOGY OF PERCEPTION (1945, English ed., 1962).

Merleau-Ponty distinguishes two aspects in which the body can be seen: in the third person and in the first person—as Sartre and Marcel do also in different terminology. The body in the first person is the lived body, which never entirely fits the objectifications of either physiology or psychology. It is the center of orientation which embraces the world. A deeper analysis shows that in this body there is a "blind adherence" (*adhésion aveugle*) to the world. Instead of disclosing the operation of a methodical ego, Merleau-Ponty sees here an area of experience that is pre-objective and at the same time pre-personal. Perception, for example, is as yet not directly a personal act. Since this perception involves no conscious attention to something outside me (where the subject is rather enveloped by, and absorbed in, the field of perception), it can perhaps be better described in terms of "it perceives in me" than of "I perceive." There is a substratum of "corporality" here, which is entirely open to the world, and from which, logically speaking, the personal "I" later detaches itself. The "history" of the "I" must therefore be seen against the background of the "prehistory" of the body as a system of anonymous functions, as the field of cohesion with the world. In his last and posthumous work Merleau-Ponty speaks of this field as a certainty which one lives, but which cannot be thought or formulated. The body is then the anonymously active intentionality which "stages" perception (*"metteur en scène de ma perception"*).

The philosophers influenced by phenomenology all use a method that is designed to uncover the hidden structures which compose the meaning of phenomena. By means of a phenomenological reduction, they discard the incidental in order to trace the logical conditions. This often leads to an analysis of the social world. Is this perhaps the field where "meanings" and "symbols" arise? It is Alfred Schutz in particular who analyzes social symbols, while Paul Ricoeur delineates language and philosophy as a "thematization" of the symbols which, in the history of human society, have served to express man's relatedness to, and contingency in, the world.

In all these analyses the theme of intersubjectivity also plays a part. So much so, in fact, that it is recognized by all thinkers to be active behind subjectivity. Sometimes, this leads them outside the sphere of personal existence, as when Merleau-Ponty founds the human person on the "prehistory" of corporality, and when Ludwig Binswanger develops in his phenomenological psychiatry the idea of the "we" as prior to personal existence ("I," "you").

Husserl had already said that what makes the human person what he is, is partly the fact that he finds himself in relation to another person, to a "you." In another philosophical tradition, that of "personalism," Martin Buber, as early as 1923, had delineated the "I-thou relation" as an essential structure of human existence. One may find many such analyses of the I-thou relation in Gabriel Marcel. But more directly associated with the phenomenological school is Max Scheler. His analysis of intersubjectivity, however, goes beyond that of Husserl's and has influenced the above-mentioned thinkers.

Scheler sees the fundamental directedness of man, not as with Husserl in the activity of reason, but in the impulse of love. He sees perceiving and thinking intentionality as rooted in a more emotional intentionality. "To know something" is a derivative form of "to love something." From this point of view Scheler develops a phenomenology of values, where values are ascribed a reality of their own. Just as in his thinking man can direct himself to set laws of thought, so as a feeling and loving being he aims at set values. This is further worked out in a philosophical anthropology where Scheler delineates in a metaphysical manner the tension between "spirit" and "life." This area of his philosophy, though important in itself, lies beyond the stricter bounds of phenomenology.

The case is different with his analyses of the social world, and of intersubjectivity in particular. He contests the idea that one begins with the knowledge of oneself and then proceeds to the discovery of other selves. The problem of the existence of other minds is a quasi-problem, in that it arises from an erroneous metaphysics. It assumes that one's "own self" is given as such. By penetrating further, phenomenological analysis shows that the concept of "I" is logically secondary and is preceded by the certainty of the existence of the other. I do not in the first place perceive only a face, nor even a facial expression, but the love, friendliness, rage itself as the way in which a fellow man reveals himself to me. Indeed, on these relations to my fellow men depends my insight into my own inner life.

This theme re-emerges in the most recent literature of phenomenology, as when Emmanuel Levinas describes the constitution of consciousness, in the theoretical as well as in the moral sense, as the confrontation with that which is *other* than myself, that is, with my fellowman, whose very existence makes a tacit appeal to me.

Brief Bibliography

T. W. Adorno, *Zur Metakritik der Erkenntnistheorie. Studien über Husserl,* Stuttgart, 1956.

S. Bachelard, *La Logique de Husserl,* Paris, 1957.

J. F. Bannan, *The Philosophy of Merleau-Ponty,* New York, 1967.

L. Binswanger, *Being-in-the-World.* Selected papers tr. by J. Needleman, New York, 1963.

U. Claesges, *Edmund Husserls Theorie der Raumconstitution,* The Hague, 1964.

A. Diemer, *Edmund Husserl. Versuch einer systematischen Darstellung seiner Phänomenologie.* Meisenheim, 1956.

J. Edie, ed., *Phenomenology in America,* Chicago, 1967.

E. Fink, *Sein, Wahrheit, Welt,* The Hague, 1958.

C. Graumann, *Grundlagen einer Phänomenologie und Psychologie der Perspektivität,* Berlin, 1960.

E. Husserl, "Nachwort zu meinen 'Ideen,' " *Jahrbuch f. Philosophie und phänom. Forschung,* vol. 11(1930); also in *Ideen,* vol. 3.

———, *Formale und transzendentale Logik,* Halle, 1929.

———, *Erfahrung und Urteil,* ed. by L. Landgrebe, Hamburg, 1948.

———, *The Crisis of European Sciences,* Evanston, Ill., 1970.

Husserl: Cahiers du Royaumont, Paris, 1959.

J. Hyppolite, *Sens et Existence dans la Philosophie de M. Merleau-Ponty*, Paris, 1963.

P. Janssen, *Geschichte und Lebenswelt. Ein Beitrag zur Diskussion der Husserlschen Spätphilosophie*, Cologne, 1964.

J. Kockelmans, *Edmund Husserl's Phenomenological Psychology*, Pittsburgh, Pa., 1967.

R. Kwant, *The Phenomenological Philosophy of Merleau-Ponty*, Pittsburgh, Pa., 1963.

———, *From Phenomenology to Metaphysics. An Inquiry into the Last Period of Merleau-Ponty's Philosophical Life*, Pittsburgh, Pa., 1966.

L. Landgrebe, *Der Weg der Phänomenologie*, Gütersloh, 1963.

Q. Lauer, *Phenomenology and the Crisis of Philosophy*, New York, 1965.

E. Levinas, *Totality and Infinity*, Pittsburgh, Pa., 1969.

W. Maier, *Das Problem der Leiblichkeit bei J. P. Sartre und M. Merleau-Ponty*, Tübingen, 1964.

M. Merleau-Ponty, *The Structure of Behavior*, tr. by A. Fischer, New York, 1965.

———, *Phenomenology of Perception*, London, 1962.

———, *The Visible and the Invisible*, Evanston, Ill., 1968.

J. Moreau, *L'horizon des Esprits. Essai sur la Phénoménologie de la Perception*, Paris, 1960.

P. Ricoeur, *Finitude et Culpabilité*, 2 vols., Paris, 1960.

A. Schutz, *Collected Papers I. The Problem of Social Reality*, The Hague, 1962.

H. Spiegelberg, *The Phenomenological Movement*, 2 vols., The Hague, 1960.

S. Strasser, *The Idea of Dialogal Phenomenology*, Pittsburgh, Pa., 1970.

W. Szilasi, *Einführung in die Phänomenologie Husserls*, Tübingen, 1959.

K. Venneslan, *Der Wissenschaftsbegriff bei Edmund Husserl*, Munich, 1962.

C. van Peursen, *Phenomenology and Reality*, Pittsburgh, 1972.

J. Wahl, *Husserl (L'ouvrage posthume)*, 3 cahiers. Les cours de Sorbonne, Paris, 1958-61.

R. Zaner, *The Problem of Embodiment*, The Hague, 1964.

Chapter Nine

From Logical Positivism to Analytical Philosophy: The Uses of Language

Logical positivism displayed at the outset (certainly if one limits it to the Vienna Circle) the characteristics of a closely knit philosophical school. In a later phase of development, however, there appeared a wide variety of insights, and one can no longer speak of a central figure, as one can in the case of the phenomenological movement. The premature death of Schlick and the geographical dispersion of the members of the Vienna Circle under the pressure of an advancing National Socialism undoubtedly were contributive factors here. There is also the fact that outstanding figures like Russell and Wittgenstein, outside the Circle, took lines of their own.

But even in the inner development of the logical positivist problematics there were occasions for divergence. We need only recall the problems earlier discussed: verification, the communicability of personal feelings, the relation between syntactic and semantic aspects of language. This development, with its growing subtlety of distinctions, is finely illustrated in the historical arrangement of a number of important texts from the works of logical positivists by A. J. Ayer in LOGICAL POSITIVISM (1959). The most marked feature, perhaps, is the turn in the thought of Wittgenstein, a turn that is also of great importance as the most influential factor in initiating the trend generally known as "linguistic analysis." This name covers a group of rather diverse thinkers who would strenuously object to being called a "school" because they show at

most a "family resemblance." It is this trend which was destined
to open new vistas for the tradition of positivism, and for the very
reason that it brought into focus the themes of "history," "fact,"
and "intersubjectivity."

Two themes serve to illustrate the further development, themes
which enter also into phenomenology, but assume there an entirely
different form: the reduction of the world to sense-data and the
linguistic character of the word "I." The structure of time, though
far less explicit than in phenomenology, enters into the discussion
of sense-data. To the question, what is real?, Kant had answered:
everything that can be thought of as existing at a particular time.
In 118 Schlick elaborated this statement of Kant by defining
verifiability—this is what he understood by the word "real"—as
the possibility of locating a phenomenon within the universal order
of time. One can only speak of a particular point in time, however,
in relation to the present. To "locate" implies that one places something in relation to the given, experienced "now" (*erlebter Jetzt*).
This method is analogous to Husserl's analyses of the function of
"now" and even more to the reduction that Carnap pursued in order
to arrive at a sphere of indubitable data, as we described in
Chapter Five. Later, Carnap rejected this "methodical solipsism"
by framing the doctrine of "physicalism." But, as an attempt at a
methodical reduction to the level of indubitable data, the conceptions of Carnap and Schlick are still of importance.

One of the differences with the phenomenological analysis is
that this "now" in the structure of time and this "*ipse*" or "self" of
methodical solipsism do not in this case lead to the doctrine of a
structural ego. This will be further explained in what follows; here
we wish to point out the affinity of this with the doctrine of sense-
data. The doctrine stems not from the continental philosophy on
which Schlick and Carnap drew, but from British empiricism.
Locke, Berkeley and Hume had themselves presented a doctrine of
sense-data. The doctrine is a recognition of the arguments of the
sceptics throughout the ages brought against the claim of human
knowledge. Doubt is dealt with methodically and thereby turned
positively into a means of finding in the content of immediate perceptions an area of indubitable knowledge.

This doctrine of sense-data has been defended by a variety of empiricist philosophers. In general it assumes the following form: propositions are so worded as to bear the incontestable form of a record of the speaker's sensations at the moment of his making the statement, (*e.g.*, instead of "I see a red house," we have the statement "I now have the impression of a red house," sometimes even ". . . of a red patch of such and such a form"). Statements about real objects in the world can be connected with these, provided they can be derived in accordance with certain rules from statements about sense-data. The logical consistency of these rules must then guarantee as large a measure of probability as possible for the final assertions about factual reality.

Two main forms of the sense-data theory can here be distinguished. First, a realist conception, in which "sense-data" is a reference to something given in reality, either by the action of objects on the knowing and perceiving subject, or by this subject selecting from available sense-data. A realist conception one would find, for example, in H. H. Price. More directly in line with the logical positivist methodlogy and as an example of pure methodical reduction is the non-realist or linguistic conception. Here it is a matter of a terminological device: statements about physical objects are translated into statements about sense-data. This conception, known also as "pragmatic phenomenalism" (Hirst), is championed especially by Ayer.

Although the sense-data theory takes its point of departure in the "now," that is, in the momentary perceptions, the structure of the sense-data is not limited to this, any more than Husserl restricted the stream of consciousness as a non-realist-psychological structure to the present. Connected with this are the rules which govern the derivability of statements concerning real objects. In the linguistic conception of sense-data, statements about momentary perceptions must accordingly be amplified by, and indeed set in the context of, statements about possible, future sensory perceptions, which can be expected on the basis of the structure of the momentary data. In other terminology, categorical material-objects statements must be translated into hypothetical sense-data statements. This linguistic operation is to be found, in some respects, already in Berkeley when he says: "The table I write on I say exists; that is, I see and feel it; and if I were out of my study I should say it existed; meaning thereby that if I was in my study I might perceive it" (PRINCIPLES, I, 3). This latter derivation according to certain rules was touched upon at the end of Chapter Six when, following Mohanty, we pointed out the analogy with the reduction of "meaning" to "capacity of words," which is in turn related to the operational method of the logical positivists.

An important aspect of this doctrine of sense-data is that it places the phenomena to be described wholly within the field of objectivity; the sense-data are simply noted, and for this special verbs are used, as when Russell uses the word "to sense." This entails the rejection of the "I," as was also the case in the doctrines of Hume and Mach. It is recognized, of course, that the "I" is a useful word in ordinary language, but not that it indicates an entity, nor even a fundamental ego. Russell, who, in a certain sense allows more scope for the "I," nevertheless criticizes the Cartesian construction of the "I" as a substance. The *cogito* of Descartes can be better defined as "it thinks in me" than as "I think," according to Russell. Carnap goes a step further when he says—it was in about 1928—that the "I" is constituted late in the stream of consciousness. He prefers therefore to reformulate the *cogito*, as Schlick had done before him, with the phrase of Lichtenberg's, much-cited in positivist circles, "it thinks." Wittgenstein also gave attention to the phrase, though his solution, as will appear, was to lie in another direction.

Separate mention must be made of the way in which this conception of the word "I" was later worked out (in 1949) by Gilbert Ryle. That the word refers to an entity is rejected by many for the reason that, as Hume had already put it, when an inventory is made of all sense-data, together with memories and the like, no special datum of experience can be found that can be specified as "I." Nor does Ryle view "I" as one datum among others, but he does ascribe to it a peculiar function. "I" is a means of pointing to other data; it is an "index-word." It is, for this reason, a mobile word, for it may be used now by one person, now by another. Ryle compares it with the word "now," which can be used at different moments. One may compare such words with bookmarks which indicate on what point one is reading. This amounts to solving the elusiveness of "I," which has been emphasized time and again in the history of philosophy, not least in the researches of Husserl and, in particular, in his self-objectifications and reiterations. For when I think about myself, I can the next moment turn my reflection on the "I" that thought about myself, and so on. This means, according to Ryle, that I comment on myself and then comment on my commentary. This is something which can also take place between two persons. In their dialogue the word "I" denotes the person commenting at that moment. In self-reflection this process occurs within the one person, but even then it is not a mysterious phenomenon or fathomless I-substance; it concerns only various indications, since the word "I" indicates each time another level of commentary. As Husserl had tried to reduce the fact of the personal "I" to the logical-idealist activity of the absolute ego, so Ryle, moving in the opposite direction, reduces the "I," in a logical-analytical sense, to a grammatical operation.

Yet, in the more recent linguistic discussions of sense-data and the notion of "I," there has been a noticeable shift of opinion. Ryle himself criticizes trenchantly every form of sense-data doctrine. A confusion has arisen here in that sensing is equated with observing something. But the sensation that takes place when one watches a horse-race is not to be equated with intuiting a sense-datum, a patchwork of colors. Linguistically, the distinction is clear if one considers that when someone looks up at a round plate held above him, he can say that this appears to be elliptical in form, but does not mean that he observes an elliptical percept, an elliptical "look." When someone notices that he is nibbling a biscuit, he cannot therefore say that he is eating "nibbles"! In point of fact, we observe the horse-race and the round plate directly and we never observe sensations as such. Ryle's criticism of the sense-data doctrine shows much affinity with Husserl's views on sensations, which as hyletic material are taken up in the intentionality of, for example, observation. Merleau-Ponty also criticizes the reduction to special sense-data, a reduction that is to be found, in fact, in Carnap's constitution of the world from simple elements. Merleau-Ponty points out that these so-called immediately given sensations are actually the result of an objectifying analysis which artificially dissects the coherent data of immediate experience. More recent work from the linguistic analysts, in particular, from Stuart Hampshire, has elaborated further on Ryle's critique in assigning to "I" a more active role in observation. This will be discussed in the following chapter, where there will appear to be on this point a still larger measure of agreement with the phenomenology of Husserl and Merleau-Ponty.

The same critique is to be found in Austin and writers influenced by him, though in a more linguistic form. It is pointed out there that one can employ statements about factual and possible perception as a means and criterion for testing the truth of statements about physical objects, though statements of the second type must not be reduced to statements of the first, since *qua* meaning they say something more. The statement "in park M there is a red house" does not mean the same as "under certain conditions it is possible to have the sensations of . . . ." Connected with this, moreover, is the whole question of verification, which we have already discussed at some length. In this connection we need only recall that Carnap had originally demanded the strict reducibility of all statements, by means of certain rules, to observable features in an empirical language. Later he broadened his standpoint, recognizing that theoretical concepts cannot be derived in this way, and spoke of rules of verification as conforming to what is taken to be normative in a given state of culture. Ayer similarly revised his position after 1946 by replacing a reduction to experiential propositions as the requirement of verification with a reduction to observation-statements, including statements of possible observation. According to his latest publications, this is to encompass more than direct verification; moreover, intersubjective statements need not refer *per se* to public objects; verifiability does not mean, further, that something must admit of being verified by *me*. Both points—the recognition of the wider horizon of statements about the physical world on the part of some, the easing of the sense-data doctrine in connection with experiences related to the historical situation and to indirect verification—point in the direction of a greater recognition of the actual, human stuation, by which the logical rules of inference have to be modified.

These shifts of opinion are to be seen against the background of developments in logical positivism: on the one hand, the study and construction of so-called artificial languages, on the other hand, the trend known as "linguistic analysis," or, more broadly, as "philosophical analysis." Carnap is associated with the first, which has been widely represented in the United States. The names of logistically orientated thinkers such as Tarski, Quine and Goodman also belong here, though these are certainly not to be reckoned as mere logical positivists. A large part is played here by semantics, which studies the relations between a "language" or system of signs and that which is signified by it (*designata*). The view that philosophy must limit itself logically to what is immediately and certainly given (such as the "stream of experience" of the earlier period of Carnap's work) is abandoned. The question of the relation with factual reality comes to the center, and while it is true that this relation is "mapped" as far as possible within a formalized language structure, it gives rise to innumerable revisions and reformulations. For the intention is to establish a system of relations between the system of signs and the data to be described in order to transpose problems from the reality of experience into those within the logical system, and there to analyze them. This has in various respects already produced valuable scientific results.

An interest in the pivotal philosophical problems, however, is alive in the other development within logical positivism, which has led to the trend of linguistic analysis. The turn to fact and to the historical world of human society is therefore the more surprising. The most important figure in this development is Ludwig Wittgenstein. Already in his first period of philosophical activity, which came to a close with his TRACTATUS, he had exercised a big influence on the members of the Vienna Circle. Even his teachers Russell and Moore felt the impact of his ideas. As appeared in Chapters Four and Five, Wittgenstein made a plea for a purely logical language, connected with the verification principle. Moreover, he held to a picture theory with regard to the relation between language and reality.

There is quite another element in his earliest thought which, though at first not so very conspicuous, has since become the subject of detailed commentary. Even in his notes of 1916 a number of metaphysical themes appear; for example, he calls that which is problematic in the world its meaning, and says that one may call the meaning of the world, "God"; to believe in a God means to recognize that the facts of the world are not the end of the matter. In the TRACTATUS he begins with the thesis that everything that can be thought can also be said, and that what can be said can be logically formulated. But *that* the world is, as we have already seen, is for him the inexpressible (*Unausprechliches*), and God does not reveal himself *in* the world. Even questions associated with human attitudes of mind—the will to improve the world, the questions of optimism and pessimism, ethics—while able to affect the limits of the world, cannot be expressed in the world and therefore cannot be spoken. These words of Wittgenstein do not entail a metaphysics in the customary sense. For metaphysics tries to put this inexpressible into the world, into words, and so becomes involved in meaningless language. Philosophy, therefore, must limit itself, if it is to solve all problems, to formulate the speakable logically. And in logic, says Wittgenstein, there are no surprises. So philosophy shows at the same time how little has been done when all problems have been solved. Therefore, philosophy will mean the unspeakable by clearly displaying the speakable.

This latter statement of Wittgenstein is in various respects reminiscent of Kant, because he too tried to safeguard logically structured knowledge by way of restricting it. The surprises of the factual world—*that* it exists, the meaning of life, the manifestation of God, the good will (ethics), the questions of life and death, in short, the resistance of the *vérités de fait*—are referred by Kant and Wittgenstein alike beyond the categories of philosophy, and by Wittgenstein even beyond the categories of language. It is in this sense that the well-known sentence with which Wittgenstein ends the *Tractatus* has to be understood: what we cannot speak about we must consign to silence.

We need to bear in mind this aspect of a "negative metaphysics" in the early work of Wittgenstein to be able to understand the transition to his later thought. This can be characterized briefly as follows. Wittgenstein abandons the ideal of the *vérités de raison* in the form of one purely logical language. Instead, he traces the various ways in which language is used within the historical forms of life. Or, as he puts it in his PHILOSOPHICAL INVESTIGATIONS: "The more narrowly we examine actual language, the sharper becomes the conflict between it and our requirement. (For the crystalline purity of logic was, of course, not a *result of investigation:* it was a requirement.) The conflict becomes intolerable; the requirement is now in danger of becoming empty. We have got on to slippery ice where there is no friction and so in a certain sense the conditions are ideal, but also just because of that, we are unable to walk. We want to walk: so we need *friction.* Back to the rough ground!" (no. 107)

This tension between what in the foregoing chapters were referred to as *vérités de raison* and *vérités de fait* is characteristic of the whole movement of linguistic analysis. As was described in Chapter Six, Leibniz could bridge the tension with his metaphysics and, in particular, with his principle of sufficent reason. He was referred by his opponents however, to the friction of fact, as when Voltaire contested Leibniz' theodicy on the occasion of the appalling earthquake in Lisbon. In a certain sense, one can view semantics, the formulated language employed by the above-mentioned thinkers, as heir of Leibniz' principle of sufficient reason, because semantics too builds such a bridge, not of a metaphysical type, but in continual revision, more liable to friction with everyday things. The more explosive problems, such as those of the meaning of the life-world, of human conflicts, of life and death, and the like appear to be able to some extent to break through the walls of the phenomenological reduction and also to evoke discussion *expressis verbis* in modern linguistic analysis.

With regard to Wittgenstein's thought, one could say perhaps that the areas of the expressible and the inexpressible, of clearly defined logical positivism and indefinable negative metaphysics, have penetrated each other—and, indeed, to such an extent that in his later work neither the one area nor the other is to be found as such. The anti-metaphysical trait is maintained, but the field of the inexpressible has become a dimension of language which has returned to the rough ground of the historical world. This can be further illustrated in a brief exposition of some of the themes of his later work.

Already in 1930 Wittgenstein had completed a manuscript in which he refers to more than one use of language as a possibility for doing justice to what is given in immediate experience. In this work, published in 1964 (PHILOSOPHISCHE BEMERKUNGEN), he even speaks of a "phenomenological language," which he sets over against a "physicalist language." The term "phenomenology" is used in physics by, among others, H. Hertz as a description of directly given phenomena. Wittgenstein has taken Hertz' mechanics in various respects as a model for certain views in the TRACTATUS (among others, his views on the network of physical language). Yet Wittgenstein employs the term "phenomenology" in his PHILOSO-PHISCHE BEMERKUNGEN in a somewhat modified sense, which is closer to the philosophical sense of the word. What is given in "physical," that is, objective space, as described by geometry, cannot, says Wittgenstein, be simply applied to immediately experienced, "phenomenological" space. Thus, for example, the field of vision, vanishing at the edge and becoming vaguer toward it, which is known in our personal, subjective experience, is not to be pictured in "physical" space by drawing the lines there somewhat vaguer or by allowing the lines to vibrate. It is here as with the relation between memory and observation, where the first is not to be pictured by rendering the second in faded colors. What is properly required, therefore, is a language of a different kind, a "phenomenological language," if the facts of experience are to have justice done to them.

At a later period Wittgenstein distinguished various "language games," which must each be seen in their own context, or surroundings, as he himself puts it. This entails a dynamic and functional view, for one can learn the meaning of words only as one traces the ways in which they function and in which they are used. Wittgenstein compares them with the tools in a tool-case. Some are very much alike, but their real significance is only apparent as the mechanic shows how one must handle them, and then it can be seen how the tools that are alike are in fact very different from each other. This can be applied in the first instance to the word "meaning" itself. Seen in isolation, this term could be thought to refer to a mysterious substance, as it were, to the "soul" of a word; this leads, however, to an impasse, because then we would be trying, according to Wittgenstein, to find for a substantive a substance. This "mental cramp" disappears as soon as one indicates the meaning in the way in which it functions in practice. Wittgenstein calls this (in about 1934, the time of THE BLUE AND BROWN BOOKS) an ostensive definition of meaning—not in the sense that one would be able to indicate an entity, a self-existent meaning, but in the sense that such an indication lends meaning to a word. The indication constitutes the meaning, so to speak, provided one remembers it is a matter of a series of acts within the world of human praxis, in which along its way such a word acquires a specific meaning. This is what Wittgenstein has in mind in his much-quoted statement: "the meaning of a word is its use."

In the varied forms of language use or "language games" and in the process of usage, the meaning presents itself. The word "brick" uttered by a brick-layer to his mate will not imply a description of a given object, but a command to fetch a nearby brick. If someone performs the actions and shows the reactions which, within the given social practice, agree with the "rules of the game" in use (with "go and sit on a 'chair,'" to go and sit on a chair and not on the floor), one says that that person understands the "meaning" of a particular word. Sometimes that could be a mistake—he performs the right action entirely by accident—but by repetition and in connection with other processes of a right use of language the certainty in this respect becomes greater. Moreover, there may occur an inner feeling of recognition of the meaning; Wittgenstein does not deny this dimension of language and rejects here, as he himself says, a behaviorist conception, by which the "meaning" would be exhausted in the ability to complete a set of operations. But this inner feeling or image, for example, of "red," where it concerns the understanding of the word "red," is never indispensable and can even be exteriorized by comparing it with the action, possible for anyone, of comparing some color in sight with a sample of color one has in one's pocket. In each case "meaning" has a social dimension, which, to be sure, does not exclude private experience, but which is never independent of it. An illustration: "I want to play chess, and a man gives the white king a paper crown, leaving the use of the piece unaltered, but telling me that the crown has a meaning to him in the game, which he can't express by rules. I say: 'as long as it doesn't alter the use of the piece, it hasn't what I call a meaning'" (THE BLUE AND BROWN BOOKS, p. 65).

Questions which have frequently arisen in philosophy, and which are answered quite positively in, for example, the work of Husserl, as to the existence of meanings, prove here to lack all sense and to be rejected as metaphysical. What receives emphasis is the necessity of indicating logical rules, which for Wittgenstein, however, are closely connected with the social context in which they are used. These rules present themselves, moreover, within a process in time, a process that one cannot cut up as one pleases. Wittgenstein provides the example of a child who must learn to read. He has printed words put before him. Suddenly he utters the right sound with the printed word that corresponds to it. Is this the moment at which he can truly read? No, it is only accidental, says the teacher, for that child has not yet reached that far. When the child gets five words consecutively right, might we say then that he can read?

Precisely because they belong to the context of a process, meanings cannot lie ready at hand. Wittgenstein devotes much attention to processes where an infinite perspective emerges. In his REMARKS ON THE FOUNDATIONS OF MATHEMATICS, in which he occupies himself with, among other things, the questions raised by Gödel, he deals with various dilemmas connected with the problem of infinity in mathematics. The difficulty already presents itself in an elementary form in extending a series. How do I know beforehand that, in the series +2, I must write 20006 after 20004, and not 20008? Indeed, how do I know that if I simply write down 2,2,2,2, etc., I must write after the five hundredth 2 yet another 2? Extending the series by +2 is no different in principle from an extension by +0. Is the meaning of "+2" and the like perhaps that I know it beforehand? One looks for a chain, opens a box and there finds a chain. Then the chain can be said to have lain there beforehand. But this cannot be compared with the instruction which contains the "+2" beforehand! The misunderstanding here is cleared as soon as one realizes that the certainty of being able to extend the series does not imply that one has already made all the steps before. Indeed, this perspective of infinity is already to be found in such ordinary questions as "how do I know that this color is 'red'?" The answer lies in practical use.

This involves far more than mere pragmatism in the sense of a reading off factual, practical use. Wittgenstein speaks about "action at a distance" (in FOUNDATIONS OF MATHEMATICS) and about "foreshadowing" (in THE BLUE AND BROWN BOOKS). Something of what Husserl called the infinity of perspectives also appears here. This action at a distance on the part of logical rules within the process of time touches also on the problems of fact. The certainty of being able to extend a series holds, but "certainly my dying first is excluded, and a lot of other things too," says Wittgenstein, as if this idea suddenly struck him. Is this a kind of joke, intended to confuse the logical and the factual possibilities? Not at all, for they are both connected, though the one is not to be reduced to the other. (What this entails will be made clear later.) Here too it is a question of logical possibilities within the factual context of rules which can hold in a human society. Therefore, the ability to extend a series is not to be conceived as simply a physical or psychological ability; it is not some hidden, mysterious faculty in man, yet on the other hand, one must say that, in the case of a parrot uttering such a formula, he can*not* extend the series. Here Wittgenstein makes use of a comparison of man and animal which had frequently been used by the philosopher and mathematician Pascal, precisely with regard to the human awareness of infinity.

Analogous to some of the criticism that was seen to have been brought against the sense-data doctrine, Wittgenstein's analyses have in view the discovery of context and perspective, and precisely in the logical rules which are operative in the temporal processes of usage. A final illustration of this must be mentioned, that of an arrow. How does one know in which direction it points? Someone accustomed to reflected images could say of two arrows set over against each other that they point "in the same" direction. But how does one arrive at the "meaning" of the arrow, above and beyond the immediate data of the chalk line or ink marks? There too something of an *ad infinitum* becomes apparent: under the one arrow one can draw more clearly a second arrow, and say, "Look, the arrow is pointing in *that* direction"; one can stand by the arrow and point in that direction with one's finger; or, to make that pointing still clearer, extend one's left hand under the pointing right hand to indicate the direction; or, must one finally take the person concerned by the hand and take him along in order to let him see what one means by a certain direction? It is clear from this example that the meaning is more and other than the material representation of the arrow; further, that this does not imply that the meaning would be something extra, an ideal arrow, as it were, drawn beneath the visible arrow, or a given arrow-meaning in the head of the onlooker. One can indeed distinguish levels of interpretation, for example, by so arranging it that one should conceive each arrow as indicating a direction opposite to that in which the arrow points. But then the ultimate meaning is the level at which one ultimately stands in the process of interpreting and handling symbols. That all this, moreover, is never entirely arbitrary appears from the possibility of "translating" the arrow symbolism into the immediate praxis of a person by taking him somewhere by the hand. With these two points, however—a level of interpretation as the point of departure for the understanding of meanings, and the connection with the praxis of everyday life—we come to matters that have to be further discussed in the following chapter: the forms of life and their implications. We must also give attention there to the place of the "I," as a level of interpretation, to which a greater structural part is ascribed by Wittgenstein and other thinkers after him, than by thinkers like Ayer and Ryle.

Brief Bibliography

J. L. Austin, *Sense and Sensibilia*, Oxford, 1962.
A. J. Ayer, *The Problem of Knowledge*, London, 1956.
———, *Philosophy of Language*, London, 1960.
R. Carnap, *Introduction to Semantics*, Cambridge, Mass., 1942.

J. Hospers, *An Introduction to Philosophical Analysis*, London, 1956.

K. Marc-Wogau, *Die Theorie der Sinnesdaten*, Uppsala, 1945.

G. E. Moore, *Some Main Problems of Philosophy*, New York, 1953.

———, "Wittgenstein's Lectures in 1930-33" *Mind*, vol. 63(1954). Also in Moore's *Philosophical Papers*, London, 1959.

A. Pap, *Analytische Erkenntnistheorie*, Vienna, 1955.

J. Passmore, *Philosophical Reasoning*, New York, 1962.

G. Pitcher, *The Philosophy of Wittgenstein*, Englewood Cliffs, N.J., 1964.

H. Price, *Thinking and Experience*, London, 1953.

G. Ryle, *The Concept of Mind*, London, 1949.

J. Urmson, *Philosophical Analysis*, Oxford, 1956.

F. Waismann, *The Principles of Linguistic Philosophy*, London, 1965.

———, *Wittgenstein and the Vienna Circle. Conversations Recorded by* Waismann, ed. by B. McGuiness, Oxford, 1967.

G. Warnock, *English Philosophy Since 1900*, London, 1958.

J. Wisdom, *Other Minds*, Oxford, 1952.

L. Wittgenstein, *Philosophische Bermerkungen*, Oxford, 1964.

———, *The Blue and Brown Books*, Oxford, 1958.

———, *Zettel*, ed. by G. Anscombe and G. von Wright, Oxford, 1967.

Chapter Ten

Linguistic Analysis of the Forms of Life

LINGUISTIC analysis breaks with the sharp bifurcation of language into that which is logically justified, that is to say, meaningful (the language of logic plus that of verification) and that which is meaningless, that is to say, which is only of emotional significance. Various writers have already described how this new movement has acknowledged precisely the multiplicity of language forms and gone on to analyze and map out the various forms of "use" and of "meaning." To this it must be added that what is involved here is both the intentionality of that which is immediately given as symbol or as word and the horizon that these words have; further, that neither of these factors concern a logical or theoretical context, but one of practical, everyday experience. This implies that the "nature" of language and, in virtue of this, the nature of things come to lie in the dynamics of human society, and thus become "history." This accounts for the fact that in many of the analytical philosophers one may come across descriptions that show a great measure of agreement with those of phenomenologists, even though, it should at once be said, the total structure of their philosophy is opposed at the central points to that of phenomenology.

In his PHILOSOPHICAL INVESTIGATIONS in particular Wittgenstein provides many examples of an analysis akin to phenomenology, because he is trying to grasp the nature, the "grammar" of certain words—"to hope," "pain," "thinking," etc.—by describing a number of concrete cases. He engages in what, in Husserlian terms, may be

146

called an "eidetic reduction," with the important difference that this in no sense intends to imply a disclosure of self-contained meanings, such as we find in the earlier Husserl, and that the meanings which become apparent in the concrete illustrations are less well-rounded and defined than is the case with the later Husserl. Wittgenstein speaks of "language games" and of "family likenesses" between words. He discovers how the meaning of, for example, an arrow refers back to the living being who makes use of such a symbol and through that use gives life, as it were, to the symbol. "Use" and "life" are often brought together by Wittgenstein. It becomes evident in all this that dualism of any kind has been rejected—between meaning and word, or soul and body, and so on—which proved also to be the case in phenomenology. When Wittgenstein points out that taste is not a mysterious factor behind the changes of fashion, and thus no attendant feeling, but rather that change of "taste" is itself the indication that fashion designers are designing differently, he offers an analysis like those one finds in phenomenologists like Merleau-Ponty. There, too, the meaning of a certain phenomenon is not something apart from the tangible data; it occurs rather in the directedness of such data within history and the life-world.

In about 1934 Wittgenstein made a clear distinction, in a certain respect, between what we have referred to as *vérités de raison* and *vérités de fait*. He distinguishes logical impossibility (*e.g.*, 3x18 inches do not go into 3 feet) from physical impossibility (*e.g.*, three persons cannot sit on this seat): the first impossibility issues directly from the "rules of play" in use, the agreements concerning units of measure, etc. Now there are some classical problems in philosophy which are in fact nothing but the confusion of the two impossibilities, such as those connected with the knowledge of other minds, and thus the problem of solipsism. For example, the statement "I cannot feel your pain" puts forward as a physical impossibility what is purely a logical one, that is, one that is implied by those rules by which the feeling of pain, *qua* meaning, is always related to me. This distinction needs to be amplified, however, in two respects. First, by the conception of "I" which Wittgenstein developed at that time, and second, by the relationship between logical language, logical norms and actual life, which he studied in his last period of activity.

If someone says, "I have tooth-ache," it is nonsense to ask him: "Are you certain that it is you who has tooth-ache?" It is a case of the above-mentioned confusion of two linguistic structures. At the same time, it is connected with the significance of the word "I," which Wittgenstein also links with the dilemmas based on the sense-data doctrine. The function of the word "I" he clarifies as follows. One can distinguish the "physical" eye from the "geometric" eye. The first is the eye to which one can point as an object among objects; for example, the eye of another or one's own eye seen in the mirror. The second is the eye with which one sees; this too one can "point to," but then in the sense that one moves one's own finger toward one's eye without it involving, in this case, the perception of the two objects that have been moved toward each other (which could be the case if one viewed the operation in a mirror). This, it will be recalled, concerns different "language games," different kinds of "grammar." The geometrical eye is not another kind of thing than the physical eye, any more than a railroad station, a railroad accident and a railroad law are different kinds of objects. Now, the geometric eye is not an object among objects, and the grammar of the word "geometric eye" stands in the same relation to the grammar of the word "physical eye" as that of the expression "the visual sense-datum of a tree" to "the physical tree." When someone points to the sun, it is erroneous to say that he is pointing both to the sun and to himself. When Ludwig Wittgenstein says "I," he is not indicating by this one person among others: "I" does not have the same significance as "L.W.," which is not to say that in such a case "L.W." and "I" mean different things, but that these words are different instruments in language.

These statements from THE BLUE AND BROWN BOOKS clarify similar considerations in PHILOSOPHICAL INVESTIGATIONS, and afford at the same time a new kind of criticism of the sense-data doctrine, in that sense-data are recognized as a use of language, and then only within the perspective of the "geometrical eye," that is to say, of the dimension of subjectivity. It now becomes clearer that, as we expressed it at the beginning of the chapter, the sphere of "negative metaphysics" and the sphere of logically restricted positivism, kept strictly apart in the TRACTATUS, now penetrate each other and so give rise to a new style of philosophizing. He had spoken of the subject in the earlier work as a "metaphysical subject," and compared it with the relation of the field of vision to the seeing eye, which cannot be seen. Just as nothing in the field of vision can lead to the conclusion that it is seen by an eye, so too, in a book that describes "the world as I find it," there is no place for the subject (TRACTATUS, 5. 631). Now, however, the portrayal has so far changed that one may perceive in the structure of the field of vision something of the non-objective eye, and that the subject is defined within the field of language. For language is now seen to be broader than the giving of information in an objective sense. In his INVESTIGA-TIONS Wittgenstein can therefore say that the statement "Only from my own pain do I know what pain is"—compared earlier in the book with a statement like "3 x 18 inches do not go into 3 feet"— is not meaningless; while, as a piece of information, it is empty, it does present a certain picture. One could say, as a provisional summary, that all expressions that picture the dimension of subjectivity are to be viewed neither as object language or information language, such as has been done, mistakenly, by traditional metaphysics, nor merely as the consequence of a number of rules or conventions about units of measure and such like, nor simply as meaningless, emotional or poetic expressions. The "metaphysical" subject (as understood in the TRACTATUS) has penetrated into workable language.

In this way Wittgenstein can steer clear of behaviorism: for it is in no sense his view that everything beyond observable behavior is a fiction; he concerns himself only with the "grammatical" fictions that arise with the problems in question. Subject language may not be treated as a kind of object language; "I" and "L.W." are different instruments in language! In the elaboration of these rules two themes are found to emerge: corporality and history. The body is considered in relation to the old problem of the identity of the person, where the answer varies according as one takes memory (here we might meet the so-called "double personality") or corporality as the criterion. The body is also to be considered in the two cases in which the word "I" can be used. Wittgenstein speaks of "the use as object" (in statements like: "I have grown six inches," "my arm is broken") and "the use as subject" (in statements like: "I have tooth-ache," "I am trying to lift up my arm"). The subjective use creates, by objective use, the illusion of a hidden, ethereal substance *in* my body. From this also it is evident that the word "I" is more than a metaphysical subject, that is, a subject outside the describable world; more too than a mere index-word that only indicates the level of commentary. Indeed, the word "I" is in a certain sense even indispensable. Wittgenstein refers to what one may call the "anonymity" of "I," which is active in every giving of a name: " 'I' is not the name of a person, nor 'here' of a place, and 'this' is not a name. But they are connected with names. Names are explained by means of them" (INVESTIGATIONS, no. 410).

There is discernible in all this something of what the phenomenologists call "intentionality," and which was illustrated in the previous chapter by the example of the arrow, made use of by Wittgenstein to show that the meaning of a phenomenon does not coincide with what is given in fact—an ink mark, for example, or, if one prefers, a sense-datum. In the above-mentioned analyses of "I" in the activities of the body, and of the references from "I" when used as a subject, this comes to more definite expression. Moreover, Wittgenstein is in search of what he himself calls a "proto-phenomenon." This is not to say that such an "intentionality" discloses something more, a special substance or an ethereal meaning. No, in the actual use of language, in the actual way in which a certain process occurs, like a person's action, there prove to be more dimensions involved than simply that which can be represented in the language of description, in object language.

When someone has a certain plan to do something, which has not yet been done by him, one can express this as follows: "He said, as it were to himself, 'I want to. . . .' " This indicates an intention, not as another occurrence at that particular moment, but as a disclosure of something over and above what actually took place at that moment. The phenomenon is comparable to the anticipation or fore-shadowing, discussed in the previous chapter, as the meaning which certain rules may have (their "action at a distance"). One can also say in this case, according to Wittgenstein, that the speaker discloses something of his inner self, not, of course, in terms of object language, as if it were a matter of a chain in a box. Once again, it is a matter of an entire process in which a particular meaning, going beyond what is actually given, becomes apparent. This is also true if one is speaking about another person. An expression such as "I meant *him*" does not refer to a particular fact, nor to a particular object. With this, a particular picture of the person concerned may, perhaps, come to my mind, but then this picture must be conceived as an illustration of a story. Only if one knows the story, does one know the significance of the picture. History is referred to indirectly here as a "story" (*Geschichte*) which has to be told; in subsequent and more far-reaching discussions of the relation of language to reality, history, indicated then by terms like "the forms of life," appears to encompass nature. This we shall now try to explain.

The changes which appear to have taken place in Wittgenstein's thought are reflected in his modified vision of mathematics. Problems with regard to the foundations of mathematics (Brouwer, Gödel) are not to be solved, in Wittgenstein's view, by reducing everything to logic. This brings him to further reflection on "measuring" and the fixation of "yardsticks." A tautology, in the sense of a composite proposition, of which the truth value is in all cases positive, also proves to be less self-evident. A tautology such as the law of the excluded middle proves to have "just as shaky a sense (if I may put it like that, as the question whether p or −p is the case" (REMARKS ON THE FOUNDATIONS OF MATHEMATICS, p. 140). That is to say, the dividing line between logical law or tautology (which is always true) and the contingent proposition (which can be true or false) is less sharply drawn, and thus here too fact is seen to penetrate into logical clarity. Or, put otherwise, it appears that logical criteria must be more flexible and be adapted to the circumstances of life.

Of the numerous discussions in which this basic idea is further worked out a few need to be mentioned in brief. A ruler embodies a system of measures, and does not represent any physical or even "ultraphysical" law. Its purpose is not to picture actual conditions, but rather to lay down a measure for facts and things. A penal code is not intended to be a description of how people in a particular country deal, for example, with a thief—it is not a work of social anthropology. Nor does it set out physical or anthropological laws: it does not say that if this happens then *that* must necessarily happen, but that if one can say that a certain number of rules are observed, *then,* given the circumstances, *that* will necessarily follow. But now, one must note, the word "necessarily" has assumed another, non-physical meaning. The same applies with respect to the "laws" of arithmetic. Just as in the first example one is not told how certain people in fact deal with a thief, but what they understand by "punishment," so in arithmetic correct answers tell us, not about self-existent, ideal laws, or about physical laws, which would be pictured in mathematics, for example, but what is understood by "counting," "units of measure," "mathematical rules" and the like.

And yet there appears in all this to be a connection with reality; not, it is true, with given laws of nature, but more in the direction in which Husserl moved in his later researches: the connection with the human, historical life-world. This comes to the fore in the following considerations. The statements "$2 \times 2 = 4$" and "people believe that $2 \times 2 = 4$" remain sharply distinguished, for only the first can be called a mathematical proposition. But what if everyone believed that $2 \times 2 = 5$? Or, what if everything one can use to help one's counting, like beans and sticks and stones, behaved in such a way that bringing together two groups of two always produced five? Two times two still equals four, but then this yardstick is at the same time unusable. Here the strict separation of logical and mathematical rules from psychological and physical processes is done away with, at least in so far as the latter become the occasion of setting aside certain standards, and, as Wittgenstein says, the setting up of a new set of rules adapted to the situation. We may now describe as "counting" what in a previous situation could not be so described.

Thus the *vérités de fait* become perceptible in the perspective of the meaning of logical rules—in the new and modified sense. The setting up of rules, the adaption of yardsticks, is no arbitrary, conventional matter. Wittgenstein speaks of "natural limits corresponding to the body of what can be called the role of thought and inferring in our life." He had already written in the TRACTATUS that the presupposition of all logical propositions is that names have significance and elementary propositions meaning; this is their connection with the world. Now, in his REMARKS ON THE FOUNDATIONS OF MATHEMATICS, he goes further: "There correspond to our laws of logic very general facts of daily experience. . . . They are to be compared with the facts that make measurement with a yardstick easy and useful" (p. 38). What, then, is the relation between logical categories and the material of empirical experience, or, in less Kantian terms, between the formation of concepts and facts of nature? In the posthumous notes published at the end of INVESTIGATIONS, he repeats that he is directing attention to the agreement between concepts and very general facts of nature, but not with the idea that the formation of concepts could be explained by this. On the contrary, Wittgenstein's conception moves rather in the direction of what, among other things, the phenomenologists refer to as "dialectic": an interplay between concept-formation and nature, between reason and fact.

Concepts, rules, systems of measurement and the like must be adapted to the empirical world; that is one side of the dialectic. What has already been observed with regard to tautologies holds good for all concepts: the criterion of identity of two data can itself be transformed in the course of establishing rules for certain phenomena. In this way, we appear to be adapting our own thought to experience. What is happening in fact is this: because we conform to certain rules of proof and of inference, our way of seeing is altered, transformed. A logical proof conducts our experience in certain channels. Wittgenstein can therefore say repeatedly that concept-formation is the limitation of the empirical. One may compare this problem-solving with a jigsaw-puzzle: the pieces do not fit together until someone shows the right pattern which the solution presents. In such a case a person's geometry is altered, so to speak, because a new dimension of space is shown him. It must be continually pointed out, therefore, that "concept," "rule," "counting," "thought" become far more elastic in this perspective, and that, on the other hand, "experience" can no longer be a fixed point of departure: even "facts," according to Wittgenstein, cannot be pointed at, but are partly determined by the methods one uses to establish "facts." Thus the conceptual forms the empirical, and the empirical calls for new concept-formation!

In view of all this, it is not surprising that Wittgenstein, like Husserl, recognizes the "truth of the market dealer" as peculiar to him. Wittgenstein speaks, indeed, only of the "shop keeper" (in FOUNDATIONS OF MATHEMATICS); on the other hand, however, this truth appears to be still more "elastic": do we come into conflict with the truth, asks Wittgenstein, if we make our yardsticks not out of wood and steel, but out of soft rubber? Can one no longer then speak of "measurement"? In ordinary circumstances we must indeed call such a yardstick unusable, but we can conceive of situations in which just this would be desired; a shop keeper could in this way treat different clients differently.

One can summarize the later phase of Wittgenstein's thought in the statement, not infrequently to be found in his writings, that verbal symbols in themselves are dead, but that their use means their life. Already in the TRACTATUS he wrote that colloquial language is part of the human organism and just as complex as that. Now, the turn in his thinking is precisely to this complexity of the living organism. He therefore describes words as a process and consequently, as he sometimes puts it, embedded in a situation. These views on "truth" and "measure" do not mean a surrender to the conventional or the arbitrary, but a recourse to the situations of life. Personal relations and the knowledge of other minds are viewed in this perspective. If one conceives language purely as description, insuperable difficulties will arise. But the perspective of the subject as the structuralization of language is already to be found in Wittgenstein's refutation of the sense-data doctrine—sense-data are rather to be compared with the "geometrical eye" and with the "I as subject." This extends still further into the perspective of intersubjectivity. It is there not a question of a description of the other, but of a concrete relation with respect to the other. "In what sense is it true that my hand does not feel a pain, but I in my hand?" is a question with which Wittgenstein touches on the problem of body and soul, and at the same time of "I." The answer lies on the practical level of encounter with other people: if a man has a pain in his hand, we do not comfort the hand, but the one who suffers and we look into his face. The conviction that my fellow man "has a soul" is not expressed in a theoretical opinion; but my attitude toward him is an attitude toward the soul. Problems about life and death, and in particular, those about the survival of the soul, have to be approached in this dimension: this "doctrine" must be conceived as a picture which does a particular service.

The soul, therefore, belongs not to the general facts of nature, but to this dimension of practical situations of life. Thus Wittgenstein points beyond natural data to the history of human society: truth and falsity rest not on a mere agreement of opinions, but on an agreement in the form of life. Elsewhere Wittgenstein says: "what must be accepted, the given, is—so one could say—forms of life." In language and its problems we are dealing not with merely theoretical questions, but, according to Wittgenstein, with deep disquietudes. Thus he can say that one can heal the sickness of a time only by a change in the mode of life, and similarly the sickness of philosophical problems only by a changed mode of thought and of life.

A characterization of the development of analytical philosophy can indicate only a few of the tendencies and must forgo a complete description. The influence of the later Wittgenstein is discernible in a wide range of thinkers, and has led to a new style of philosophizing. The line of logical positivism has been most faithfully pursued where philosophers have worked with the basic ideas of neopositivism that we discussed earlier, and have applied them to the more recent developments in science. In addition, an evident empiricist trend continues alongside an on-going operational approach to theoretical concepts. Among philosophers who have published sometimes important works in this area are H. Feigl, E. Nagel, W. Sellars and B. F. Skinner. R. Carnap and others, as we earlier pointed out, have trodden new ground by their study of semantics and the framing of artificial language. The group of philosophers, finally, who following Wittgenstein, have developed linguistic analyses or, more broadly, analytical philosophy, present the greatest variety of opinion and the most radical transformation of the positivist tradition of thought. From the broad field of their activities we shall trace but a few characteristic paths.

A dominant position in this development has been occupied by J. L. Austin. His philosophy is in fact an analysis of language—so much so that the question has arisen among his pupils as to whether one would not do better studying philology than philosophy. On his own account, Austin would like to get rid of a part of philosophy by turning it into a science of language. On the other hand, his linguistic analyses open up new philosophical perspectives as he shows how questions of fact in daily experience penetrate the structure of language. That refers not only to his critique of the sense-data doctrine. The tension between logical clarity in language on the one hand and the complexity of the situations of life on the other makes it less easy than logic would like it to decide whether a statement is true or false. One must sometime be satisfied with the question whether the statement is fair, whether it is a proper thing to say. This must not, says Austin, be conceived in a pragmatist sense, for it is a matter of realizing that language is not first of all descriptive, but the doing of action. Pure description and theoretical statements come later and are connected with the development of science. Even pure statements must be studied "in a speech situation," because even then one wants to "do things with words."

Austin develops this argument, very much in line with Wittgenstein, by devoting special attention to language in which an action is performed, as, for example, "I thee wed," "I do," spoken at the marriage service. He terms such sentences "performatives" as over against what he calls "constatives"; the question 'true or false?' is not applicable here; we must ask whether or not it is appropriate, or serious, whether it is fortunate or goes wrong, and so on. In short, Austin here recognized the "complexity" which is characteristic of life and truth and things. "It's not things, it's philosophers that are simple." We must therefore be prepared to revise our scheme of language and to reckon with all kinds of odd situations. And an unsettling, contingent illustration: "Is Mr. Smith at home?," as a question to which one can answer neither "yes" nor "no" if it happens that Mr. Smith has just died. An associated thinker, John Wisdom, uses a similar example and provides as an answer "He is elsewhere," an answer which cannot be dismissed as metaphysical or absurd, or as a joke, because it expresses in words an "old hope."

Austin's approach opens possibilities for a philosophical ethics, which neither he nor Wittgenstein developed. Various writers have analyzed the language of ethics, some by reducing it to a language of exhortation ("this action is good" is not description but exhortation), others in a more penetrating way by distinguishing the many shades of language, which point toward ethical rules that are connected with irreducible human decisions and attitudes; a pure conversion into the language of exhortation would make ethics a language of propaganda. These views are expressed in various ways by R. M. Hare, C. L. Stevenson, Stuart Hampshire and others.

This concrete world of action and responsibility is brought clearly into light from yet another viewpoint: the position of "I." Austin, like Wittgenstein, points to the asymetrical structure of language: "I wed" as a "performative" is a different use of language than "he weds," which is a "constative." The problem of other minds, investigated at length by Ayer, among others, as a positive possibility for verification, as also of ascribing to oneself a set of descriptions belonging to another, acquires here a new dimension. Wisdom had discovered something of the fear of, and impulse toward, the otherness of the other, but had spoken further of the dilemma implied in the knowledge of others' feelings. Austin goes further, because one cannot use the verb "to know" descriptively, thus with an object. One may recall what Wittgenstein had said on the *attitude* to the other. P. F. Strawson, similarly, offers far-reaching analyses on this point as he indicates the asymmetry of the first and the third person: "N is depressed" means that N's depression is observed, not experienced, by the other and that, at the same time, N's depression is experienced, not observed, by himself. If one fails to accept this structure—this ambiguity, Merleau-Ponty would say—of our actual language, then one cancels one of the terms and so become either a sceptic with respect to the existence of other minds or a behaviorist.

Strawson distinguishes the concept of "person" as a primitive concept, which cannot be further reduced, for example, dualistically to soul and body. The pure ego or consciousness points to the "person" as an elementary datum in language and the life-world.

Strawson points out, precisely as Max Scheler on this point, that from this concept of person it is quite unnecessary to argue analogically in regard to other minds. For in order to ascribe experiences to myself, I must be able first to ascribe experiences to others. This structure of intersubjectivity is significant in another respect. The problem of the identification of a person, and indeed of every concrete datum, can be posed as follows: Is it not possible for a second, completely similar constellation to exist? Not if one notices that the one who describes a system himself occupies a particular position in time and space and so himself provides a reference point which individuates the network. Strawson sees this "individuation" as accentuating the location of a phenomenon in a "story" and further in a "history." Words such as "here," "now," "I," "you," therefore, not only belong to the personal sphere, but also provide an intersubjective and public reference-point. In this way, Strawson indicates the transcendental function of subjectivity.

Much the same thing is to be found in the comprehensive discussion of Stuart Hampshire on the function of the ego. With Wittgenstein and Austin he points out the asymmetry of language with respect to the first and the third person. "I know what he now wants" is a proposition with uncertainty as to the content on grounds of inadequate information. "I know what I now want," however, is *not* a proposition, but an indication of an intention of the subject; Hampshire speaks here of a non-propositional, intentional statement. This is connected again with a basic feature of consciousness which is inseparable from action: as the body always occupies a particular position, so consciousness is always the envisaging of possibilities. The word "intentionality" occurs frequently with Hampshire, and while it is true that this is not understood in the phenomenological sense—it is not an activity constituting meanings —it qualifies "consciousness" as directedness.

A number of other, important analyses ensue. First, that culture, symbols and language can never be analyzed in themselves, but only within the context of that which man envisages: man is an "intentional animal." Second, that it is by this intentionality that man takes his bearings in the world. Deeper than communication in language is the "act of intentional pointing, away from himself and towards an object." In a kind of "phenomenology of observation" Hampshire shows how action and observation are complementary and how man is both "the person as observer" (among things) and "the person as agent" (as changing relations). This implies, thirdly, the corporality of man. Pointing is pointing away, in which "I" indicates the same place as my body. Every identification of an object and thus every statement and verification with regard to external phenomena presuppose a "situated consciousness," that is, as a body among others, finding itself in a "now." A fourth point is the critique of the sense-data doctrine which follows from this. Sense-data, according to Strawson, are not basic, since their identification rests on the identity of "persons to whose histories they belong." Hampshire links this with the bodily position of the person and consequently with the dimension of the subject, as in their own way Wittgenstein and Austin had also argued. Hampshire develops this in a doctrine of perspectives which shows great affinity with the *Abschattungen* of Husserl and Merleau-Ponty. Forms of language like "this is a so-and-so" and "this looks like so-and-so" ("sense-data grammar") point to the changing relations of the bodily observer to the object, so that the external object can be looked at from more than one point of view, can never indeed be observed in all its attributes at the same time, so that in every statement about an object a step is taken from the aspect of that object to its identification as an object of a certain kind.

Finally, we may summarize these analyses, and those of all the thinkers mentioned here, with Hampshire's conclusion that description is essentially inexhaustible and that the limitation of a conventional system of symbols is determined by natural limits, which are connected with the interests of society. A theory of descriptions, such as Russell framed, independent of the intentions of the speaker is impossible. Statements, which include an expression like "the contemporary king of France" or a word like "God" can only be assessed within a concrete frame of reference, where attention must also be paid to ontological references. Hampshire therefore allows linguistic analysis only as a clarification of the anthropological concepts that one already employs and must employ. In the study of man, as distinct from the animal, one must take into account his varying social patterns and consider his history, if new distinctions are to be made.

Brief Bibliography

E. Albrecht, *Sprache und Erkenntnis. Logisch-linguistische Analysen*, Berlin, 1967.

J. L. Austin, *Philosophical Papers*, Oxford, 1961.

——, *How to Do Things with Words*, Oxford, 1962.

A. J. Ayer, *The Concept of Person*, London, 1963.

M. Black, ed., *Philosophical Analysis*, Ithaca, N.Y., 1950.

J. Evans, "On Meaning and Verification," *Mind*, vol. 62(1953).

H. Feigl and W. Sellars, ed., *Readings in Philosophical Analysis*, New York, 1949.

A. Flew, ed., *Logic and Language*, 2 vols., Oxford, 1952 f.

M. Furberg, *Locutionary and Illocutionary Acts. A Main Theme in J. L. Austin's Philosophy*, Göteborg, 1963.

P. Geach, *Mental Acts*, London, 1959.

S. Hampshire, *Thought and Action*, London, 1959.

J. Macmurray, *The Self as Agent*, London, 1957.

W. Quine, *From a Logical Point of View*, Cambridge, Mass., 1953.

R. Rosty, ed., *The Linguistic Turn. Recent Essays in Philosophic Method*, Chicago, 1967.

G. Ryle, *Dilemmas*, Cambridge, 1954.

E. Specht, *Die sprachphilosophischen und ontologischen Grundlagen im Spätwerk L. Wittgensteins*, Cologne, 1953.

P. Strawson, *Individuals. An Essay in Descriptive Metaphysics*, London, 1959.

B. Williams and A. Montefiore, ed., *British Analytical Philosophy*, London, 1966.

L. Wittgenstein, *Philosophical Investigations*, Oxford, 1956.

——, *Remarks on the Foundations of Mathematics*, Oxford, 1956.

A Final Confrontation:
The Transcendental and the
Linguistic Approach

Phenomenology and analytical philosophy are two characteristic movements in contemporary philosophy which also exercise influence outside philosophy in a particular style of scientific reflection. One meets in psychology, the social sciences, medicine, aesthetics mutually divergent conceptions which are closely connected, respectively, with phenomenology and analytical philosophy. This contrast can be viewed in some respects as a difference in intellectual "climate": one could even locate this climate geographically by speaking of continental as over against Anglo-Saxon thought, although these geographical demarcations, as we have already explained in Chapter One, are not to be taken as definitive. One could also speak of a difference in mentality: phenomenology appears to recognize rather more irrational elements (intuition, imagination) and to be more metaphysically disposed than the modern exponents of positivism. All this requires an investigation into the philosophical status of the movements concerned, in so far as that is possible within this mutual confrontation. In this way, onesidedness of one kind or another can be shown to be just that. It can be seen, moreover, that it is more than a question of a psychological difference of mentality, or of the gravitation of certain traditional contrasts in the history of philosophy. More important still, we have noticed that within the divergency of the two most important currents of contemporary philosophy a certain convergency began to be manifest. Not in the sense of a kind of compromise, but in the sense of a development which was a reaction to similar questions discovered by each of the schools within the field of their presuppositions.

The contrast between them has in no sense been erased. Even now one may typify them by calling phenomenology the philosophy of subjectivity and analytical philosophy that of objectivity. These designations must be understood in a technical sense; subjectivity does not mean an emotional attitude, directed to itself, but a method which analyses objective structures from the position of the subject, for which these structures are given as such. Objectivity does not mean a superficial attitude which relies purely on objective statements, but a method which tries to describe structures unambiguously, not excluding those phenomena which present themselves with man (consciousness, intention, saying "I," etc.). One can also formulate the contrast in terms which are perhaps most applicable to the earlier development and which we employed in Chapter Six in an initial confrontation: phenomenology reduces operations with logical rules to the meanings to which they are directed; neo-positivism reduces meanings to the logical operations by which they are defined. The latter we can also express by accentuating a tendency and qualifying neo-positivism as behaviorist and operationalist. In the same way we can see phenomenology—even though this is expressly rejected by Husserl—as idealism in a Platonic sense. In the later development of phenomenology, it is true, meanings are withdrawn into the hidden, though traceable, activity of the ego, but then one may speak with even more justification of an idealism, now in a non-Platonic sense. Thus, roughly defined, the contrast results in: idealism (subjectivism) versus linguistic behaviorism (objectivism).

The contrast is to be thought of as a "model," intended to make possible a finer characterization, so that insight may be gained into the more central features of the ideas and developments of the schools concerned. To do this we must look at two things: first, the similarity of methodological approach which is apparent within varying tendencies of these philosophies; second, the surprising fact that both schools contrive to escape the ultimate consequences, in the sense of extreme formulations, even though they find themselves, so to speak, in the magnetic field of idealism and linguistic behaviorism respectively. If one is prepared to typify the schools in terms of these extreme positions one must also say, within this model, that they shrink from the consequences of them. In both cases this leads to a more open methodology, by which fact makes an entry and loosens the logical rigidity of each of the systems.

The resemblances we have been able to refer to again and again. However different their points of departure, both philosophies concern themselves with what is immediately given. To this extent both movements are anti-metaphysical, in that any interpretation *a priori*, that is to say, prior to any possible investigation of the phenomena, is rejected. While it is true that Husserl distinguishes self-contained rules and truths, and that the logical positivists proceed with the distinction between tautological and verifiable statements, even this *a priori*, which in both cases is disclosed only by way of immediate data, is abandoned. The later distinctions (which continue to echo the earlier ones), namely, the transcendental ego with Husserl and the criterion of the appropriate use of language with the linguistic philosophers, are rather dimensions of a whole field of investigation from which they can no longer remain in isolation. Connected with this is a distinction between classical metaphysical systems like idealism and materialism on the one hand, and phenomenology and neo-positivism on the other. The first of these present a closed system, which is either in fact complete or can in principle be completed.

Husserl had often said, what in fact he put into practice, and even repeated shortly before his death, that he must really start all over again! This is not peculiar to the person of Husserl, but, as will presently become clear, is inherent in the whole phenomenological method. The same phenomenon is to be found with other phenomenologists. Merleau-Ponty was occupied, just before his death, with revising the fundamental theses of his philosophy. In thinkers as diverse as Scheler, Ricoeur and Thévenaz one meets thorough revisions and transformations of their own thought. The same can be said of various neo-positivists. Carnap has occasionally revised his whole philosophy; Wittgenstein even interrupted his philosophical work for a considerable time to resume it in an entirely new way. This gave rise to a development of thought which prevented it from lapsing into an exclusive school and a dogmatic dismissal of other opinions. This development is connected with certain tendencies in the analytical methodology which have been conducive to greater flexibility and to closer adaptation to the historical character of human society.

In the first instance, the rejection of a metaphysical *a priori* on the part of the schools concerned is possible because they want to develop a strict logical system—the word "logical" appears frequently in the titles of works by Husserl, Carnap and Wittgenstein —and at the same time to make that which is positively given, which as phenomena presents itself, the point of departure of their philosophy. This means for the logical positivists overcoming the traditional weakness of the empiricists in the analysis of logic and mathematics. The original interpretation of the latter as tautological structures and the description of a logical law as a tautology (Wittgenstein) could then be considered by Schlick, with some exaggeration, as the most important advance in the history of philosophy.

The reverse is the case with Husserl when, against a background of continental idealism and neo-Kantianism, he returns "to the things themselves." This is not, to be sure, a return to material, or even actually existing, objects, as we have already seen, but concrete phenomena do provide for Husserl the touchstone of his theoretical constructions. Husserl at one time called himself, as previously cited, the true positivist. Recent interpretations of Husserl also emphasize this feature. Thus Mohanty sees in Husserl a Platonism of "meanings," interlaced with a positivist doctrine of the fulfilment (*Erfüllung*) of the intentional act, a point to which Findlay also refers and which he himself elaborates in his philosophy. W. Szilazi characterizes Husserl's phenomenology as a transcendental positivism. H. Plessner tells us how Husserl once said to him that he had always sought reality; and how Husserl, in saying this, gave graphic expression to both intentionality and its fulfilment by hitting his walking stick against the doorpost.

In this agreement too the differences between the schools are still apparent. This can be formulated as follows and the extreme qualification—idealism versus behaviorism—to some degree corrected. The recognition on both sides of the logical element and the positive empirical element takes place in phenomenology, initially, in dualistic terms, in that meanings appear to be timeless and thus, in this respect, are set over against the empirical status of phenomena. This reminds us of the old dualistic doctrine of man as body and soul. It is theoretical analysis then (as in science, for example) which discovers meanings. Logical positivism, on the other hand, reminds us rather of a monistic conception, in that "meanings" are restricted to the use of meaningful language, which is governed in turn by logical rules (of a tautological nature, or as directives for verification statements). Phenomena themselves are translated into such language, whether the experimental language of Carnap or the language of physicalism, or reduced from object language to sense-datum language, and so on. This reminds us of the old philosophical doctrine of man which reduces the soul to the physical.

The comparison with dualism and monism in the doctrine of man is a way of showing how, from different viewpoints, a convergence is possible. One meets this in the history of the concept of man when man is defined as a living being, in the intentions and possibilities of his life, by which the dualistic conception is given greater unity, in so far as living, corporeal man displays a unity of physical and psychic aspects. A materialist conception of man is then broken through when man is considered more as what is factually given, in that he sets himself purposes and views himself and the world in terms of future possibilities and tasks. Now, this can serve to illustrate the way in which a dualism and a monism of meanings are broken through, so soon as phenomenologists and logical positivists introduce the idea of "life" for the interpretation of phenomena. Then meanings can no longer be separated in any respect from the field of the life-world, nor living language be reduced to the language of logical use.

Husserl, in his later work, often compares the relationship between the structure of "I" or ego and the world of phenomena with that between life and the organism. The variety of forms and the structures of development of the latter are only to be understood in terms of the organism as a *living* whole. He tries therefore to demonstrate how the structures of science and logic fall back on features of practical life. What is often described as an *a priori* structure Husserl sees as a result of idealization, that is to say, as an expression of the possibility of induction and prediction on which, he says, all life rests. The concept of "reason" itself, so often in philosophy made an independent entity and thus into a storehouse of *a priori* concepts, becomes with Husserl a dynamic and dependent factor, which qualifies the activity of the ego as an historical development like that, in particular, of European culture. "Reason" has less of an *a priori* character and is more open to historical renewal. It denotes therefore not so much a description of something as an appeal to something. Theoretical reason becomes practical reason, which then, however, is more closely connected with "life," that is, with the life history of society, than it is in the case of Kant. "Reason" thus becomes a designation of an historical language, a call to overcome intellectual fatigue and to integrate all scientific reflection at the level of the transcendental. In the later Husserl, therefore, mathematics is no longer the discovery of self-contained truths, but the invention of truths appropriate to the situations in the life-world.

Wittgenstein moves from logically restricted language to ordinary language, which in his TRACTATUS he called as complex as the human body. In FOUNDATIONS OF MATHEMATICS he compares an artificial language with a trumpet, which only by means of an attachment or mouth-piece can be brought into contact with the human body and thus to its application. The mathematician, says Wittgenstein, is an inventor, not a discoverer. What he means by this becomes clear if one recalls his ideas on "measure" and "yardsticks," which brought to light the connection between general situations of life and the choice of particular yardsticks and methods. Some considerable time before, F. P. Ramsey, in his study on the foundations of mathematics, had in some respects pointed in the same direction. He had then, in agreement with Schlick's conceptions, defined the laws of nature, not as propositions that admit of being either true or false, but as directions, instructions, which are necessarily required for the framing of such propositions.

Wittgenstein emphasizes the directives situated in the forms of life. Here, for him, lies the horizon which is decisive for the manner in which everyday language functions. Here too is the context of Wittgenstein's often-used picture of signs, which in themselves are dead, but by use alive. Independently of Wittgenstein, Merleau-Ponty also makes use of the tool-picture to explain the meaning of words: only through its use does one know the meaning of a tool. Wittgenstein's view must not be conceived, as we explained in the preceding chapter, as an operational doctrine of meanings. For the word "use" indicates precisely a "transcendence in immanence," that is to say, it points to the fact that language is to be understood neither in terms of words nor in terms of operational rules, but in terms of its total connection with the most general facts of nature on the one hand, and with the historical forms of life on the other.

For phenomenologists and analytical philosophers alike the picture of life, with its variety and flexibility, has had the effect of checking tendencies to dogmatism or simplification, which could have led to a dualism or monistic reductionism. "Meanings" are a reference to life as it expresses itself in language. The nature of this life is interpreted variously. With the phenomenologist it is the activity of the transcendental ego or of pre-objective corporality; with the analytical philosophers it is the vitality of the various forms of life, in so far as these are part of the praxis of human society. Both, however, come together in this, that this life is more than what is given in immediate experience. This applies also, as we have already noted, with respect to "use" as the life of words. One must not take this to mean, according to Ryle, actual "usage," which is determined by custom, fashion, tradition, etc. "Use" means that there are certain rules, "rules of the game," as there are rules for the use of a tennis racket. Thus it goes beyond "utility" and is, moreover, connected with "interpersonal" rules (Ryle).

The angle of vision one adopts by preferring the greater complexity of what is referred to as "life" to the simpler, but one-sided constructions of dualism or reductionism has a significant consequence. An important place is given in their discussions to "models," which, in this connections, are to be understood as the use of concepts, diagrams and images enabling us to conceive the aspect of reality being investigated. It requires a great simplification of the data, but it is just this that makes it possible to work with the model and handle it as an instrument in the continuing investigation. This concept of model is now being used in a number of sciences, both social and natural. A model is then to be clearly distinguished from a picture. It is a restricting and grouping of data, but according to a clear method, so that it should rather be called interpretation than picturing.

To find a philosophical foundation for the concept of model has been the concern of the philosophers here discussed. Wherever life is found, it is crystallized in forms and structures, but without ever being exhausted in them. Life is not, therefore, an additional substance, but the "narrative" of ever-new, often unpredictable forms. All this applies equally, in both schools, with respect to meanings, as manifest in language, symbol and culture. From this point of view, all yardsticks and operation rules, all scientific concepts and logical structures, by which language is in certain respects fixed, acquire the character of "models." The difference with the previous period of logical positivism is precisely that all this was not then qualified in terms of "model." In the most recent development, philosophers who devote themselves entirely to the study of artificial languages are perhaps most in danger of regarding constructions of this kind not as models but as a solution to the problems of reality and life. But even they have given some reflection to the meaning of the model in science, and, more comprehensively, to the range of their own logical concepts. Ryle has sharp words for those who fail to recognize these restrictions. He speaks of the "dream" of those who suppose that the formalization in a logical calculus from non-formal concepts of ordinary language can solve all problems and logical perplexities. But the unscheduled forces of everyday discourse "are not reducible without remainder to the carefully wired marionettes of formal logic" (ORDINARY LANGUAGE).

This recognition of a stubborn remainder that cannot be formalized is the insight into *vérités de fait* which, with constant vitality, breaks open the structures of the *vérités de raison*. Ryle therefore says that chess can be of great use to generals, but can never replace the winning of a battle, any more than philosophy is finished with counting. We may say, similarly, that the "laws of nature" will never be able to explain the whole of history, but have rather the function of a model. The above-mentioned conception of Ramsey moves in the same direction, and in Wittgenstein it is even clearer. In his TRACTATUS he uses the picture of a network, of which the panes may or may not be made black when it covers the whimsically formed field behind it, i.e., actual reality. The network as such tells us nothing about reality, the laws of nature nothing about nature; only that this particular network fits better than another. It is still a question here of the comparison of a logical frame with nature. In the later work there is a shift from nature to history, which means that the logical frame cannot be used in simple black and white terms, to indicate what is true and false. The model character of the frame then comes to the fore. Sometimes Wittgenstein speaks of the handling of yardsticks as belonging to the "natural history" of man, a more biological term which still lies, as it were, between nature and history. But then Wittgenstein became increasingly concerned with the role the particular signs can play in the situations of life. And when he uses the term "forms of life," as we argued in the previous chapter, he is meeting with the irreducibility of human history and its ever-changing structures.

The model is well illustrated in the picture of a map which is made of landscape in order to facilitate our orientation, and precisely by way of methodical restriction and schematization. The picture is already implied in Wittgenstein's discussions and has been worked out by many others. Ryle has objections to the designation "linguistic analysis," since "analysis" carries undertones from the science laboratory, with its marshalling of natural data and its well-rounded conclusions. He would rather compare the philosopher with a cartographer than with a chemist, since the problem area of philosophy is unlimited. This means also that there are different kinds of maps according to the demands of the situation. Austin speaks of the global character by which a particular schematic map may be appropriate for a general but not for a geographer, and here again statements concerning truth and falsity fall back on the question of whether something is the proper thing to say. What we referred to above as the shift from nature to history can also be expressed, therefore, in terms of a move from descriptive language to language by which one commits oneself. The model-character is then the more clear, because it is not only a question of schematization and quantitative restriction, but also of qualitative transformation: from language of commitment to descriptive language. These ideas are extensively developed, with the model-character of scientific mapping also in view, by M. Polanyi, a philosopher outside the neo-positivist tradition and who may be said to occupy a position between phenomenology and philosophical analysis.

Husserl too, in his later period, portrays natural science and logic as models of reality and as theoretical concepts derived from the pre-theoretical praxis of the life-world. Instead of the discovery of a physical reality behind the reality of everyday, science is a coat of ideas thrown over the everyday world. Of great significance in this connection is the work of Scheler, even though this stems from an earlier phase of the phenomenological movement. Within the analytical tradition the insight into the model-character of unequivocal, logically formulated language signified the broadening of language in general, because description was seen against the background of the language of commitment. In the previous chapter we noted the importance of this for the language of ethics. Scheler's doctrine of self-existent ethical values falls entirely within the frame of Husserl's earlier phenomenology, but his doctrine that knowledge is never a self-contained process, but proceeds form a participation by love in that which is known, is extremely important and relevant. The more so in that he is more radical here than the analytical philosophers in so far as he conceives every description and interpretation as rooted in the pre-theoretical *ordo amoris*. He can thus pronounce the problem of the knowledge of other minds a quasi-problem, in view of the fact that it is only by the participation of the other in myself that self-knowledge is possible: this is therefore logically posterior. With Merleau-Ponty this participation is more impersonal and his description of the "prehistory" of "I" has proved to give rise to difficulties. On the other hand, he presents a more scientific analysis of scientific knowledge, which he compares very often with maps which facilitate orientation in the landscape, but which can never, of course, supersede it. He emphasizes the ambiguity of initial experience, while the maps, the languages of science may only portray objects when purified from all equivocation.

Both schools of thought point to the model-character of systematized knowledge. If this appears to be a form of relativism, that is not in fact the case. The value and certainty of logical and scientific knowledge is not at all being called in question, but rather being restricted. Such knowledge is not made relative so much as relational, that is to say, related to the wider contexts from which this knowledge itself has arisen. But it is precisely in this that the value of theoretical schematization becomes evident, because this becomes an instrument for the total orientation of man. According to some, this applies also to philosophy itself. Wittgenstein in the TRACTATUS describes philosophy as a praxis, and one which brings clarification. Later he comes to see it as more far-reaching; while retaining the function of mapping the various problems, rather than of solving the problems of life, it can now identify these problems as "deep disquietudes" behind the complications of language.

Three points need to be added to this. First, that in these parallel trends in the two philosophies the divergence is also expressed. The restriction and, at the same time, the recognition of logical and theoretical language are supported on different grounds. In analytical philosophy the starting-point is still of a linguistic nature. This is to say that the models of science are made relative by the analysis of other, multifarious forms of language, against which the above-mentioned methodical restriction can stand out. In this respect the positivist tradition is preserved: the later development does not mean that philosophers are now moving into other fields of philosophical research, such as the hunting grounds of metaphysics, but that their insight and outlook have become more sensitive and varied. In the phenomenological movement the point of departure is a transcendental one. "Transcendental" is evidently not equivalent to "transcendent"; it signifies the conditions without which the structures being investigated would not logically be possible. The conditions are never ready to hand and cannot then be discovered by a particular science—to suppose that they could be would lead only to psychologism or sociologism or the like. For this reason it is understandable that neo-positivism, from its own point of view, should label this transcendental standpoint (though unfairly) meta-physical. This applies to the function of the ego in Husserl, to the later ideas of Scheler on the function of mind in the phenomena of the human world, to the role of the irreducible, pre-theoretical relatedness with the world in Merleau-Ponty. The reproach is justified in so far as it is inconceivable that the philosopher should see a transcendental starting-point which no one else sees.

The second remark concerns a point of agreement. The analyses of the life-world and of forms of life and the recognition of the model-character of purely theoretical schemes provide a new, more dynamic vision of "facts." We have seen repeatedly how various thinkers view facts as more than what is merely given. Facts are themselves the result of the operation of natural and historical data on the one hand, and of concept-formation on the other. Wittgenstein puts this briefly in the statement: "The limit of the empirical is concept-formation." In this respect one could call Wittgenstein's doctrine a "transcendental lingualism," as Stenius expresses it in speaking about the TRACTATUS. Husserl points out that the things called factual are influenced by far less factual data, namely, value-objects in the world of human culture, such as paintings, statues, houses, etc. Linguistic analysts in the narrower sense show how the language which lays down facts ("constatives") arises from a wider use of language in which the element of performance and of persuasion is central. This common trend can perhaps be summarized as follows: statements that something is the case—sentences with the word "is"—proceed from statements indicating that something ought to be the case—sentences with the word "ought." Differently expressed, "facts" are linked with "values."

A third and final point is that in both schools of thought everyday reality is described as inexhaustible. The "etcetera" belongs to the essence of the thing, says Husserl. The perspectives show "transcendence in immanence" in the sense that every apprehension of a concrete object points beyond itself to other possible ways of approach. Even in thinkers within the neo-positivist movement who follow the classical form of logical empiricism or proceed to the construction of artificial languages and semantic systems, this recognition can be found. A great variety of artificial languages is possible, each language having a limited validity by its methodical restriction of infinite possibilities to a finite series. Behind logical systems lie decisions which explain why such-and-such a system was chosen. For some the decisions themselves can only be explained on pragmatic grounds, in terms of utility in connection with a given, practical situation, though these grounds would only become apparent as and when expressed in theoretical language (*e.g.*, one in which one situation is weighed against another). This line of thought is variously developed by L. J. Cohen, H. Feigl and W. V. Quine. The line of the later Wittgenstein appears clearly in Stuart Hampshire when he judges every description inexhaustible and typifies every conventional system of symbols by its limitation. In reality there are no constants as such or natural types for identification, but every conceptual re-arrangement of data contributes to the constancy of the field of perception.

The common trend in contemporary philosophy, as sketched in the preceding paragraphs, does not at all point to a more irrationalistic way of thinking. The stress on the inexhaustible character of everyday language and the life-world prevents philosophy from becoming, in Wittgenstein's words, an engine turning idle. Philosophical investigations must analyze everyday language and behavior. This can be done also from a purely logical point of view, especially when new logical tools are constructed for the analysis of practical and moral behavior; as is done in various ways by Carnap, Bar Hillel, Stegmüller, Quine, Morris, von Wright and Apostel when they develop, for instance, semantics and a deontology. The lines of recent developments in both phenomenology and linguistic analysis are pointing in the direction of further research into the life-world.

This Husserlian concept strongly resembles Wittgenstein's "forms of life." Both concepts refer to a more practical and more historical horizon which provides the contextual framework for any analysis of meaning and of logical structures. Thinkers like Hampshire, Strawson, Toulmin, Ricoeur, Merleau-Ponty and Levinas, to mention only these, are developing the concept of such a life-world in widely different ways. This leads to many points of contact with the evolution occurring in various scientific disciplines. For example, the concept of "structure," as used in linguistics and cultural anthropology, can be considered to be a result of logical investigation, applied to the directly given, historical world. Claude Lévi-Strauss analyzes in this way the world of myths and the patterns of kinship in various societies. Against a background of lived, mythical experience distinctive features and structures are delineated and logically—even mathematically—interrelated.

I learn the meaning of a word, writes Merleau-Ponty, as I learn the use of a tool, by looking at it in the context of a certain situation. Such a sentence could also have been written by a linguistic analyst. The concepts of the "anonymous ego" in Husserl and of a more logical "I" in Wittgenstein and Ryle are now operating within concrete contexts. Man thus becomes a bodily being acting within a psychologically and sociologically definable situation, from which human language—including the languages of logic and science—draws its meaning. Logical validity is no longer an eternal essence, nor the mere acceptance of rules by a community, but related to "intersubjectivity" in a more historical sense. For phenomenologists as well as analytical philosophers "meaning" and "truth" are co-determined by factually lived reality.

Thus a final confrontation between both trends of thought can be expressed as follows, putting the accent on the problems which are now coming into view. One way of describing traditional metaphysics is as an attempt to throw a bridge between the *vérités de raison* and the *vérités de fait*. Metaphysics in this sense is expressly rejected by both trends. Originally they went for purely logical research, discarding the analysis of factual reality or trying to incorporate it in the logical network. Here the continental and the Anglo-Saxon traditions clash, because phenomenologists try to derive logical functions from meanings, and logical empiricists to derive meanings from logical operations. But a convergency comes into play, which draws them back from the extremes of idealism

and operational behaviorism and which consists precisely in the
vérités de raison being forced open by the *vérités de fait.*

The differences between them prove to be in no sense wiped out.
The transcendental approach of phenomenology is to start with
positive and concrete data and to reach down to depths, with the
attendant danger of abstruseness; Husserl compares his philosophy
with archaeology and Merleau-Ponty speaks of pre-history. The
linguistic approach of logical positivism, similarly starting with
positive and concrete data, is to aim at breadth, with the attendant
danger of a voluble superficiality; the analysts compare their work
with that of the cartographer. A widening of boundaries under the
pressure, the friction of fact is nevertheless discernible in both. This
brings into view at the same time the life-world, ordinary language, in short, the history of human society with its decisions and
evaluations. In logic there are no surprises, writes the earlier Wittgenstein. The later development is the process of learning the
language of surprises. That the world is and that the life of the
human mind is as it is now become visible in phenomenological and
linguistic analysis.

All this leads to tensions. What is most fascinating in the converging tendency of these, in many respects, diametrically opposed
trends of thought is that the issue has not been another systematic
rounding off of ideas, but a renewed posing of questions. Even
the transcendental reflection on the ego has as its vocation, according to Husserl, to clarify the meaning of this actual world and of
its task. The tension in his own philosophy is particularly sharp, so
that he may well be accused of a certain inconsistency, were this
not so closely associated with the attempt to do justice—without
building a bridge with the *vérités de raison*—to the surprising
presence of the *vérités de fait.* The basic tension in the later phenomenology can be defined, with Ricoeur, as that between the
"life-world" and the constituting activity of the ego; or, with
Landgrebe, as that between the insight into the historicity of subjectivity and the necessity for an absolute foundation for self-
reflection.

In Wittgenstein, Austin and others there is an analogous tension,
which is more linguistic than transcendental: the confusions in-

herent in human praxis and the necessity of clarifying and justify-
ing utterances in language. Here too the tension is insoluble.
Wisdom speaks of "paradoxes" that must be given expression, and
Ryle of the "systematic ambiguity" which requires that words pre-
serve a certain elasticity and that meanings be not established beforehand. The word "ambiguity" is to be found also in Merleau-
Ponty in connection with the tension between language (with the
inclusion of theoretical concepts) and reality (with him, that of
openness to the world). Wittgenstein, on the same grounds, rejects
both finitism (in mathematical logic) and behaviorism (in the
doctrine of man): "Both deny the existence of something, both with
a view to escaping from a confusion." The unsettling factuality of
the questions of life and death prove to be traceable to some extent
with phenomenologists and analytical philosophers. The clarification and limitation of meaningful language brings Wittgenstein to
raise problems like this: "If in the midst of life we are in death, so
in sanity we are surrounded by madness" (MATHEMATICS, p. 157).

We are dealing here with tensions that have also been discussed
by existentialists. Yet it would be a mistake to set phenomenologists
and analytical philosophers in this light, as has been done, for
example, with Wittgenstein in a German introduction to his works.
For we are not at all concerned with a philosophy that takes
existential commitment, guilt, anxiety, death, etc. as its themes. On
the contrary, such realities of life penetrate, as appalling and sometimes surprising elements, into the positive praxis of providing
clarification. These tensions do not mean the rupture or failure of a
methodical and positive philosophy; but, within the field of problems, they bring to light something of mystery—to use the
terminology of Gabriel Marcel, which has been applied in Anglo-
Saxon philosophy by M. B. Foster. It is more correct to see this
tension (as in both schools a greater methodical flexibility becomes
evident) as a new range of problems. What we described above as
the *vérités de fait* forcing their way into the *vérités de raison* must
now be defined more carefully. For it is not merely a question of
recognizing facts which had at first been overlooked. No, these very
facts prove to be the result, on the one hand, of the forms of life
presenting themselves, and the other hand, of methodical opera-

tion. "Facts," as we put it, proceed from "values." These values must not be conceived as entities, but as tendencies, evaluations, commitments and moral-religious persuasions within the history of the human community. "Nature" is embraced by "history." Put differently, the language of surprise proceeds from the tension between the necessity of an absolute foundation and clarification on the one hand, and the recognition of unexpected, significant events on the other. The problem now is that of the "genealogy," of the logical connection between, "facts," "values" and "events."

The metaphysical bridge enables one to close a philosophical system. It may then lay claim to an absoluteness which, when placed in the history of thought, cannot be honored. The philosophical method employed by phenomenology and logical positivism makes an attempt to do away with metaphysics. Various writers have been able, it is true, to point to the implicit metaphysics to be found even in logical positivism and linguistic analysis. But both movements are trying to transpose this into a new dimension in which words and things and facts are described. Seen in this light, the above-mentioned tensions are hardly incidental; they are essential to this style of philosophizing. Both schools are more and more aligning themselves with history, moving in the lines displayed by concrete events. There is no talk here of a bridge, but rather of a "third dimension" (to use Husserl's expression) which comes to light in the reflection on "fact," "truth," "life-world," "commitment," etc.

All this implies a new form of self-reflection. In this respect phenomenology, with its transcendental analyses, has made an important investigation, for which the neo-positivist tradition offers far less scope. The factuality of nature and the life-world not only entails dilemmas in language, but also raises problems about the speaker, the "I," the active reason. A transcendental analysis can only be preserved for an idealist substantialization if the factuality of the historical and social (intersubjective) world, if "event" refutes the claim to the absoluteness of the "I." The essential limitation of man as subject itself calls for a use of language which is more than merely logical or merely indicative. Husserl speaks, in his manuscripts dealing with ethics, about the good as a more intensive reality. In the Anglo-Saxon tradition G. E. Moore as well as many contemporary analysts occupy themselves with this intensification of reality. Connected with this are what we have spoken of as "transcendence in immanence," the connection of facts with values, of "constatives" with "performatives," and of models with a language of commitment.

Whitehead, in his metaphysics which is related to the natural sciences, describes the event, among other things, as a spatio-temporal unit. The same term, but now transferred from nature to history, is to be found in a phenomenologically-minded thinker, Pierre Thévenaz (*événement*). But here the event calls for such a transcendental openness that the thinker himself must become a problem for his thought, and finds his freedom in renouncing every metaphysical absolutism. Such an intensification of the transcendental dimension of investigation into the concrete "I" of the speaker or writer goes beyond the work of Husserl, though Husserl, to be sure, emphasizes the third dimension of reality and the life-world as a correlate to a renewal of human self-reflection.

We have previously compared Husserl and Wittgenstein with respect to the absolute ego as idealistically conceived, which can only be called real, however, in self-identifying reflection (reiterations) in concrete, historical men. Wittgenstein had earlier spoken of a metaphysical "I," that is, one beyond the reach of meaningful language, while later this "I" becomes the condition of giving names, in language. More recent analytical philosophers have further elucidated the connection of the subjective pole of the structure of language, the "I," with the concrete unity of the physical and psychic as an agent in the affairs of life. The new problems that are now emerging signify also a new beginning for further investigation into the forms of language, social patterns, ethical decisions, the integration of model and theory within wider horizons. In the midst of a continuing divergency between phenomenologial and logical positivist traditions of thought the convergencies are all the more striking and significant, and precisely because they give rise to further progress of philosophical investigation. The point has been made arrestingly and tersely by a philosopher of the logical positivist tradition. F. Waismann portrays philosophy as an activity which is more than the analysis and critique of language, in that it brings deeper insight. The function of philosophical arguments is that they undermine existing categories; they are never, therefore, logically compelling—they go beyond the well-trodden paths of existing logic. Philosophy can thus enable us to see things in a new light. Waismann connects this explosive function of philosophy with freedom: logic compels, philosophy sets us free! ("How I see Philosophy," in CONTEMPORARY BRITISH PHILOSOPHY).

This statement is quite in harmony with Wittgenstein's thought when he writes in the FOUNDATIONS OF MATHEMATICS, for example, that to resolve philosophical problems one has to compare things which it had never seriously occurred to anyone to compare. Thus philosophy, in the phenomenological and analytical movements alike, becomes something like a gate of invasion through which reality makes surprise attacks, breaking into language, and making history within the walls of scientific and logical thought.

This appears also from the many discussions, to which we have already alluded and which are still in progress, about the distinction between analytic and synthetic propositions. The distinction is no longer maintained in terms of sharp separation. Whether or not a statement is analytic depends on the logical system in which it arises; in the history of science certain synthetic propositions have appeared, for example, which at a later stage of development could be derived without the intervention of empirical facts, directly from basic rules. But the reverse also occurs with an unexpected combination of empirical facts (one might examine the possibilities of originally analytic propositions like "all celibates are unmarried," and "all Indians live in India"). Writers of various persuasions, including some outside the analytical movement, have contributed to this new line of reflection: M. White, W. V. Quine, W. Sellars, M. Bunge, L. J. Cohen, H. Delius, R. Haller. The distinction in question, according to these writers (in spite of their differences), is "contextual" and "gradual." This is to say that unexpected, empirical comparisons can break through the traditions of language, and that, further, the advance of scientific methods now comes closer to logical research and forces it into dynamic tension. Put more concisely, *vérités de fait* become the motor for logical rules in their further construction of *vérités de raison*.

To this it must be added at once that the factual, far from being fixed, must be constantly redefined and re-evaluated. It has been one of our concerns to show this connection of "facts" with "values." When Wittgenstein, for example, interprets mathematical proof as a decision to adopt a certain line of procedure, he is committing himself to the doctrine that one can never point one's finger at facts, but must consider how they come to be established. This is argued on a broad front by Gellner in his challenge to linguistic analysis in the narrower sense. "In fact 'analyses,'" he writes, "almost always plainly do have evaluative implications." He sees philosophy as making explicit what is implied in ordinary language, as to some extent influenced by the natural and social sciences.

In short, neither facts nor logical rules are prior to the act of "picking out." They interact. *Vérités de fait* and *vérités de raison* together form the mobile field of the history of language, thought and science, a history which is closely connected with human action, persuasion and evaluation. Toulmin advocates a "comparative logic," on the analogy of a comparative anatomy of living beings which is not to be applied uniformly in every area. This means at the same time, he says, the re-introduction of historical, empirical, and even anthropological considerations in a philosophy which tries to be *a priori*. Recent phenomenology has been practising just this kind of comparative analysis, bearing in mind the variegated material being presented by sciences like psychology and cultural anthropology. The *rapprochement* between Husserl's "pure grammar" and the empirical sciences which was advocated at the time by Bar-Hillel is beginning to be realized in the work of phenomenologists and of scientists who are in some way associated with phenomenology, such as L. Binswanger, F. J. J. Buytendijk, M. Dufrenne, A. Gurwitsch, R. Ingarden, E. Minkowski, A. Schutz, G. Bachelard, C. Lévy-Strauss, R. Ruyer, Mircea Eliade, E. Gendlin, R. May.

We now come to a final summary. Phenomenology and the analytical trends alike arose out of dissatisfaction with over-speculative philosophy, which threatened, moreover, to be swallowed up in purely psychological argumentation. Both disengaged themselves from merely factual research so as to withdraw to the domain of purely logical analysis. They stood, nevertheless, at opposite poles. For phenomenology sought for a super-personal evidence of meanings as the source of logical operations, whereas logical positivism saw these impersonal, logical operation rules as the origin of meanings. It was in this contrast, however, that the initially concealed presuppositions of both parties came to light. They tried, each from their own philosophical tradition, to free themselves from the grip of recalcitrant facts and events. But the separation between *vérités de raison* and *vérités de fait*, and between analytic and synthetic propositions, and the more deep-seated insulation of logic against praxis, and of pure description and indication (statements with "is") against persuasion and evaluation (statements with "ought"), proved to be untenable. A new freedom in philosophizing was acquired by comparing familiar things and events in an unfamiliar way. Despite ineradicable differences, the movements have come to show common tendencies, and it is not without significance that Husserl calls himself the true positivist, and that Wittgenstein sponsors a "phenomenological language," or that Austin defines his philosophy as a linguistic phenomenology. For there is a concern on both sides for phenomena, for the story in which facts and logical rules act and react on one another.

How is this to develop? We can already begin to see the *rapprochement* with the empirical sciences. The new and often surprising material of modern cybernetics, biology, cultural anthropology, historical studies, etc. is raising new problems and could engender, in both cases, a tactical overhaul of philosophical method. On the other hand, this development entails a prospect for "metaphysics"; not in the sense of a speculative system, but in the sense of a reconsideration of the problem of factual existence, of the "that" of reality. That movement which is devoted to the continuation of logical positivism in the construction of symbolic logic and semantics, and in the application of artificial languages is obviously less interested in these questions. Over against this, linguistic analysis, in virtue of its interest in the logical rules of ordinary language, has the advantage of being better able to confront (often concealed) ontological and metaphysical problems, and in so doing to leave less scope for others to construct speculative systems without logical, empirical or phenomenological discipline.

In the most recent developments of phenomenology and analytical philosophy, one field of research has been cleared, so to speak, with two focuses: the new empirical data of the sciences on the one hand, the fundamental question concerning the "that," the contingency of facts and events on the other. The classical problems of existence, essence, creation, time, discussed by such thinkers as Plato, Augustine, Berkeley, Leibniz, Kant—to mention only these, cited frequently by both schools of thought—is leading again to renewed philosophical activity. It has become evident, moreover, that these questions are to be answered not merely in descriptive or indicative terms—that would only lead to speculative metaphysics—but also in terms of other, variegated forms of language, such as those of evaluation, persuasion and commitment.

The development of philosophy has not come to an end. Perhaps, after the phase we have just sketched, there will come a period of over-preoccupation with the success and technique of a particular science. This would happen, for example, if philosophy became absorbed in the argumentation of biology or of the social sciences. The moment will come when philosophy reacts, as at one time phenomenology and logical positivism reacted against psychologism and behaviorism and endeavored to frame a logically pure and incontestable method. Then again this will be a kind of *"reculer pour mieux sauter,"* a purification which occasions a new insight into the factual world and its phenomena. But this will happen only if thinking men remain sufficiently alive and sober to view the old world with new eyes.

Brief Bibliography

Analytic Philosophy. La Philosophie analytique, Colloque de Royaumont 1960, Paris, 1961.

K. Apel, *The Development of Analytical Philosophy of Language as Related to the Problem of "Geisteswissenschaften,"* Dordrecht, 1967.

A. Ayer and C. Taylor, ed., "Symposium on Phenomenology and Linguistic Analysis," *Proceedings of the Aristotelian Society*, Suppl. 33(1959).

L. Bejerholm and G. Hornig, *Wort und Handlung. Untersuchungen zur analytischen Religionsphilosophie*, Gütersloh, 1966.

G. Bergmann, *Logic and Reality*, Madison, Wisc., 1964.

L. Cohen, *The Diversity of Meaning*, London, 1962.

H. Delius, *Untersuchungen zur Problematik der sogenannten synthetischen Sätze a priori*, Göttingen, 1963.

M. Dufrenne, *Jalons*, The Hague, 1966.

——, *Language and Philosophy*, tr. by H. Veatch, Bloomington, Ind., 1963.

L. Eley, *Die Krise des Apriori in der Phänomenologie Edmund Husserls*, The Hague, 1962.

J. Feibleman, "Antifactualism," *Philosophy and Phenomenological Research*, vol. 25(1964-65).

J. Findlay, *The Discipline of the Cave*, London, 1966.

M. Foster, *Mystery and Philosophy*, London, 1957.

G. Funke, *Phänomenologie—Metaphysik oder Methode?*, Bonn, 1966.

H. Gadamer, "Die phänomenologische Bewegung," *Philos. Rundschau*, vol. 11(1964).

——, *Wahrheit und Methode*, Tübingen, 2nd ed., 1965.

E. Gellner, *Words and Things*, London, 1959.

G. Janoska, *Die sprachliche Grundlagen der Philosophie*, Graz, 1962.

H. D. Lewis, ed., *Clarity Is Not Enough*, London, 1963.

R. Martin, *The Notion of Analytic Truth*, Philadelphia, Pa., 1959.

J. Mohanty, *Edmund Husserl's Theory of Meaning*, The Hague, 1964.

M. Polanyi, *Personal Knowledge*, London, 1958.

W. Quine, *Word and Object*, Cambridge, Mass., 1960.

I. Ramsey, ed., *Prospects for Metaphysics*, London, 1961.

P. Ricoeur, *Histoire et Vérité*, Paris, 1955.

G. Ryle, "Ordinary Language," *The Philosophical Review*, vol. 62(1953).

——, "The Theory of Meaning," *British Philosophy in Mid-century*, ed. by C. Mace, London, 1957.

—— and J. Findlay, ed., "Symposium on Use, Usage and Meaning," *Proceedings of the Aristotelian Society*, Suppl. 35(1961).

S. Shoemaker, *Self-knowledge and Self-identity*, London, 1963.

C. Smith, "Conscience et positivisme," *Revue de Métaphysique et de Morale*, vol. 69(1964).

J. Staal, "Analycity," *Foundations of Language*, vol. 2(1966).

C. L. Stevenson, *Ethics and Language*, New Haven, Conn., 1945.

S. Strasser, *Phenomenology and the Human Sciences*, Pittsburgh, Pa., 1963.

P. Thévenaz, *L'homme et sa Raison*, 2 vols., Neuchâtel, 1956.

————, *What Is Phenomenology?*, ed. by J. Edie, Chicago, Ill., 1962.

Thinking and Meaning. Entretiens d'Oxford, Louvain, 1963.

F. Tilman, "Phenomenology and Linguistic Analysis," *International Philosophical Quarterly*, 1966.

S. Toulmin, *The Uses of Argument*, Cambridge, 1964.

C. van Peursen, *Body, Soul, Spirit*, London, 1966.

F. Waismann, "How I See Philosophy," *Logical Positivism*, ed. by A. Ayer, Glencoe, Ill., 1959.

W. Walsh, *Metaphysics*, London, 1963.

M. White, *Toward Reunion in Philosophy*, Cambridge, Mass., 1956.

Index of Names

Adorno, T., 129
Albrecht, E., 160
Alson, W., 55
Anscombe, G., 72, 145
Apel, K., 182
Apostel, L., 173
Aristotle, 47
Asemissen, H., 115
Augustine, 105, 182
Austin, J., 20, 21, 100, 136, 144, 156-160, 169, 175, 181
Ayer, A., 59, 70, 72, 80, 81, 96, 97, 131, 133, 136, 144, 157, 160, 183

Bachelard, G., 19, 180
Bachelard, S., 129
Ballard, E., 116
Bannan, J., 129
Bar-Hillel, Y., 74, 93, 99, 102, 173, 180
Barnays, P., 19
Barone, F., 81
Beard, R., 82
Becker, O., 42, 47
Bejerholm, L., 183
Berger, G., 55, 102
Bergmann, G., 183
Bergson, H., 71, 106
Berkeley, G., 15, 26, 106, 122, 132, 133, 182
Biemel, W., 27, 116
Binswanger, L., 128, 129, 180
Black, M., 72, 160
Blanshard, B., 102
Boehm, R., 102, 116
Bolzano, B., 24, 38, 42, 65, 120
Brandt., G., 116
Boyce-Gibson, W., 55
Brentano, F., 21, 23, 25, 27, 32, 33, 39, 67, 106
Brouwer, L., 151
Buber, M., 128
Bunge, M., 179
Buytendijk, F., 180

Cairns, D., 116
Carnap, R., 25, 58, 60, 64, 66, 67, 69-82, 86, 93, 95, 101, 105, 107, 108, 123, 132, 134-137, 144, 155, 163-165, 173
Churchill, J., 56
Claesges, U., 129
Cohen, L., 173, 179, 183
Comte, A., 20
Conrad-Martius, H., 103
Copi, I., 82
Cowley, F., 102

Delius, H., 179, 183
de Muralt, A., 56
Descartes, R., 12, 15, 33, 51, 54, 134
de Waelhens, A., 56
Diemer, H., 129
Drüe, H., 102
Dufrenne, M., 180, 183

Eddington, A., 71
Edie, J., 129, 184
Eigler, G., 116
Eley, L., 183
Eliade, M., 180
Embree, L., 116
Euclid, 64
Evans, J., 160

Farber, M., 42, 116
Feibleman, J., 82, 183
Feigl, H., 82, 155, 160, 173
Fels, H., 42
Findlay, J., 19, 88, 164, 183
Fink, E., 55, 102, 105, 129
Fisch, I., 42
Fischer, A., 130
Fleischer, M., 116
Flew, A., 160
Foster, M., 176, 183
Frege, G., 23-25, 27, 31, 36, 48, 57, 58, 60, 65, 66, 72
Freud, S., 68
Funke, G., 183
Furberg, M., 160

185

Index of Subject Matter

Knowledge, *a priori* and *a posteriori* aspects of, 18; logical, 64 f.

Language, philosophy of, 26, 45 ff., 156; formalization of, 73 ff.; protocol and system, 74 ff.; and reality, 77 ff., 99 ff.; uses of, 131 ff., 163, 167; games, 140 ff.; performative and constative, 156 f.; everyday, 166 f. See also *Analytical Philosophy* and *Linguistic Analysis*.

Law, physical, 70 f.; logical, see *Logical Structures*.

Life-world, 97, 104; horizon and, 149; and forms of life, 172.

Lingualism, transcendental, 172.

Linguistic Analysis, 16, 20 f., 69 ff.; and forms of life, 146 ff.

Logic, interest in, 25 f.; pure, 47; of classes, 57 f. See also next entry.

Logical Structures and Empirical Data, 23 ff., 29 ff., 59 ff., 73 ff., 91 ff.

Love, 170.

Mathematics, 151 f., 166.

Meaning, 24; phenomenology and, 29 ff., 54 f.; logical positivism and, 57 ff.; operative or intuitive, 83 ff.; independence of, 95; and language game, 140 ff.

Metaphysics, 12, 51, 59 f., 98 f., 106, 122, 138 f., 149, 163, 177.

Method, transcendental, 53; of phenomenology and logical positivism, 83 ff.

Methodology, as feature of phenomenology and analytical philosophy, 12, 83 ff.; of science, 13.

Model, 167 ff.

Neo-idealism, 11.

Neo-Kantianism, 11, 22, 164.

Neo-positivism, 20, 95, 162.

Neo-Thomism, 11.

Nominalism, 15.

Nonsense, sense and, 46, 60; and counter-sense, 74.

Objectivism, 162.

Perception, 32, 39 f., 50, 81.

Person, concept of, 157 f.

Personalism, 128.

Phenomenology, analytical philosophy and, 11 ff., 83, 161 ff.; and metaphysics, 12; structural features, 12 ff.; tension in, 17 f.; history of term, 19 f.; descriptive, 22; and meaning, 29 ff.; description of, 37, 140; as rigorous science, 33; of the ego, 103 ff.; of life-world, 117 ff.; final confrontation with analytical philosophy, 161 ff.

Philosophy, analytical, see *Analytical Philosophy*; phenomenological, see *Phenomenology*; two poles of contemporary, 11 ff.; existential, 11, 19, 118 f., 125, 176; of science, 11; positivistic, 12; see also *Positivism*; methodology, 12; and geography, 13 f.; transcendental, 16; and science, 37; and analysis, 37; normative, 67 f.

Physicalism, 78 f.

Poles, subjective and objective, 16 f.

Positivism, 14, 19, 22, 56, 57; logical, 20, 25 f., 31, 78, 81, 96, 155, 175; and meaning, 57 ff., 83 ff.; from logical, to analytical philosophy, 131 ff.; transcendental, 164.

Pragmatism, 15 f., 143.

Probability, 84 f.

Propositions, synthetic and analytical, 61, 90 ff.; analysis of, 68 ff.

Psychologism, 24, 29 ff., 35, 62, 85, 92.

Psychology, 22 ff., 29.

Questio iuris and *Questio Facti*, 17 f.

Rationalism, 15.

Realism, 14 f., 22, 48.

Reason, 118, 166.

Reduction, phenomenological, 22, 49 ff., 103, 126 f.; and factual existence, 44 ff.; eidetic, 44, 103; analytical, and factual existence, 73 ff.

Reiterations, 114.

Resemblance Between Phenomenology and Analytical Philosophy, 12 ff., 18 ff., 161 ff.

Science, 30, 41, 120, 170; and philosophy, 37; phenomenology as science, 83.